GLOBAL PANEL®

MEETING THE WORLD IN PERSON

The Prague Society for International Cooperation

present

The Series of Public Policy Sessions:

NEXT STEPS TO A FREE CUBA

Learning from the Peaceful Revolution in Central Europe

Berlin

Federal Republic of Germany

LAS GRANDES CAUSAS
REQUIEREN GRANDES SACRIFICIOS

Preface

After the Cold War many communist countries transferred to democratic rule. One of the few exceptions is Cuba. Cuba was at the center of the worst military crisis during the Cold War. In 1962 the USA faced down the Soviet Union. The two world powers came to the brink of war over the deployment of nuclear weapons on the island. Since then the USA has boycotted Cuba politically and economically. In December 2014 the US and Cuban government surprisingly announced the resumption of US-Cuban-relations. Because technology is moving so quickly – faster than political institutions react – the USA and Europe have been forced to adapt. Their cooperation is a necessary part for the political and economic transformation of Cuba. Considerable attention is being paid to determine what democratization in Cuba would include. Human rights, the rule of law and elections are small pieces of the puzzle. The Global Panel Foundation and The Prague Society for International Cooperation are committed to bringing people together to discuss and broaden our knowledge. We will use our experience to apply new concepts and frameworks for sustainable development in Cuba. During a series of public policy sessions in Berlin,

Germany, diverse groups of Cuban human rights activists and dissidents, politicians, businessmen and academics were brought together. They discussed concepts, frameworks, cases, tools, and the best practices to cope with the emerging challenges to Cuba.

Building on the foregoing, this work collects contributions by authors covering Cuban as well as Central European perspectives. As the development in Cuba is relatively new, a range of articles was received. These cover a wide variety of subjects. After the public policy sessions, the keynote speakers were asked to provide their manuscripts for the publication. These manuscripts and articles are arranged in order to provide some structure to guide readers. The articles have been grouped into six parts according to the schedule of public policy sessions: Cubans meet Bundestag; Leadership in Cuba; Lessons learnt from 1989/90; The Cuba Strategy from a German perspective, and Cuba from a Czech and Latvian perspective. Initiatives for Change in Cuba close the publication. This work gives an outlook for further activities relating to democratize Cuba. Undoubtedly there are other ways that the articles could have been grouped. We think this grouping made the most sense.

Cubans meet Bundestag

Katharina A., Research Associate of a German MP, summarizes the talks with members of different human rights groups from inside and outside Cuba. These groups formulate the hope for sustainable transformation and change in communist Cuba. On the other hand, they ask for participation of civil society in the transformational processes with the Cuban government.

Leadership in Cuba

As the title of this part implies, leadership is essential for Marxist-Leninist regimes. They live on centralized authority and autocratic leadership. Santa Coloma, a journalist and former personal translator to Fidel Castro, identifies in "*The Castro Clan – An obstacle for a Cuban reform process*" the logic of the Cuban leadership circle since the Cuban Revolution – and its willingness to protect its benefits in the future despite progress in reforms.

Lessons learnt from 1989/90

In the following chapter historical developments and experiences from an East German dissident's perspective are in the focus. Reinhard Weißhuhn, Robert-Havemann-Society, presents *"Human rights in the German Democratic Republic and Hungary"*, an analysis about the birth of the Helsinki agreement in 1975 and the effects on the dissident movement in Central Europe. It exemplifies the situation in Eastern Germany and Hungary until the fall of the Iron Curtain.

The Cuba Strategy from a German perspective

In this chapter, the question arises, which strategy and means are necessary to start a transformation of the Cuban political and economic system. Markus Meckel, the first and last democratic Foreign Minister of the GDR, discusses the German point of view in *"Cuba strategy: Design for a social democratic position determination"*. It decribes important elements of a strategy and of essential means to achieve progress in the Cuban system.

Cuba from a Czech and Latvian perspective

Dr. Martin Palouš, Deputy Foreign Minister (Ret.), starts his lecture with a dialogue between two icons of the Czech and Cuban freedom movement: Vaclav Havel and Oswaldo Payá.

In his chapter *"The unfinished dialogue between Vaclav Havel and Oswaldo Payá. Cuba in 2016"* he describes the developments since the Prague Spring, the Helsinki Conference and the Velvet Revolution. He builds a bridge to the Cuban developments in 2016 finalizing with a positive outlook for the coming years.

Oskars Kastens, former Latvian Minister for Social Integration, presents *"Eastern European lessons for 'Freedom Island'"*, an overview about the democratization 25 years after the fall of the Iron Curtain. He summarizes three recommendations for Cuban democratization: supporting disenchanted Cuban society groups and engaging Cuban elites in international organisations; accessing development assistance programs by EU and USA, and a more proactive role by the Catholic Church as an independent player.

Initiatives for Change in Cuba

This part focusses on important and sustainable initiatives, which influence the transformation and change in Cuba. Dr. Martin Palouš introduces *"The Role of Vaclav Havel Legacy Institutions in the Current Cuban Debate and The Proposed*

Cuba-Related Activities in 2016". These initiatives and activities underline the relevance of the transformational processes in Cuba.

Boris Luis Santa Coloma proposes in his *"Radio Cuba Dialoga"* a dialogue and information platform. Hana Jakrlova presents her initiative *"Cuba: Before the Dawn"*, which is an art project reflecting on Cuban reality through works of independent Cuban and international artists. The project covers several exhibitions presenting photography, multimedia and conceptual works, as well as performance and book publications.

The book "Next Step to a Free Cuba" is of use to policy makers, NGOs, academics, and practionners who are starting to project what Cuba will need for democratization, modernization and international cooperation.

Remarks:

Some of the chapters in this volume are also published in German and Spanish language. The chapters exclusively reflect the views of the authors.

Table of Content

Table of Captions

Part I: The Series of Public Policy Sessions

Part 1: Cubans meet Bundestag

What Cubans do report about!

By Katharina A.

The representatives of several Cuban dissident and human rights groups have unanimously reported that since the "opening", the regime celebrates a revival and feels more recognized internationally.

The number of short-termed arrests of opposition members and human rights activists has rapidly increased since December 2014. The reasons for this development are on the one side that the regime wants to show force and on the other side that more people are ready to talk openly. They all have reported about threats, humiliations or even about discrimination of their kids concerning their school and university education. Some of them have suffered violent attacks, too.

They have positively assessed the opening and the international talks. But they have asked for Germany's influence in a way that

1. the human rights are playing a leading role on the agenda during the talks with the Cuban government and
2. the "inofficial" civil society is actively involved and heared.

Additionally, they have requested to set a focus on the situation inside the Cuban jails. The conditions there were described as catastrophic, not only for political prisoners.

The courageous and sometimes risky commitment of the present representatives of civil society to human rights in Cuba is impressive. One representative from Miami concluded what would be most important regarding the negotiations with the Cuban government:

"Empowering the people, not the government!"

Worüber Kubaner berichten!

By Katharina A.

Die Vertreter von verschiedenen Dissidenten- und Menschenrechtsgruppen berichteten einhellig, dass seit der „Öffnung" das Regime gleichsam auflebe und sich international wieder mehr anerkannt fühle.

Die Zahl der kurzzeitigen Festnahmen von Oppositionellen und Menschenrechtsaktivisten habe seit dem Dezember 2014 stark zugenommen. Dies liege zum einen darin begründet, dass das Regime Härte zeigen wolle, und zum anderen daran, dass mehr Leute den Mund aufmachten. Sie alle berichteten von Drohungen, Demütigungen, z.T. Benachteiligung der eigenen Kinder bei der schulischen Weiterbildung bzw. Studium. Teilweise erlebten sie auch gewalttätige Attacken.

Sie bewerten die Öffnung und die internationalen Gespräche prinzipiell positiv. Sie baten aber, dass gerade Deutschland darauf hinwirke, dass

1. die Menschenrechte einen sehr prominenten Platz in den Verhandlungen mit Kuba einnehmen und
2. auch die „inoffizielle" Zivilgesellschaft mit eingebunden und angehört wird.

Außerdem lautet eine Bitte, auch die Situation in kubanischen Gefängnissen zu betrachten, da die Zustände nicht nur für die politischen Gefangenen wohl katastrophal sind.

Es war beeindruckend, mit welchem Mut und mit welch hohem persönlichem Risiko diese Menschen in Kuba für die Menschenrechte eintreten. Ein Vertreter aus Miami zog das Fazit, was angesichts der laufenden Verhandlungen mit Kuba wichtig wäre:

„Das Volk stärken, nicht die Regierung!"

Part 2: Leadership in Cuba

Boris Luis Santa Coloma: The Castro Clan – An obstacle for a Cuban reform process

I remember the first time I met Fidel Castro Junior. It was in 1962. An old friend of my father – a former guerrillero – brought him to us. I found his manner interesting, typical of people accustomed to be the center of everything. I tried to impress him and showed him my comics – Superman, Tarzan, etc. Instead of praising me, the eldest son of Fidel Castro told me to throw away this "American garbage". In 1962 nobody could imagine that this young anti-imperialist could one day become a defender of a Cuban opening for American capital. Fidelito – little Fidel – or José Raúl – his alias for people closest to him – inherited his father smartness. Fidel junior grew up under the tutelage of his uncle Raúl Castro and the personal care of José Abrahantes, the head of Fidel Castro´s bodyguards. It seems he was predestined to a higher position in the Cuban nomenclature, but one day Fidel Castro condemned his mentor Abrahantes to prison. Fidelito – in a gesture of loyalty - defended his protector – the only one person who cared for him all of the years when his father was busy creating guerrillas all over the world. Castro punished his own son and Fidelito lost his privileges. Since then, the eldest son of Fidel has gravitated in the orbit of his uncle Raúl Castro. At the moment, he is his adviser for European issues.

Using a network of ghost companies, the Castro Clan acquires a fortune. But his real power doesn't emanate from their financial or economic resources, but rather from their strategical position in the Cuban society. The Castros are the main link for a continuity of the Castrismus – Fidel´s own interpretation of socialism. The Castros – like modern-day Borgias – have taken key positions under their control. The eldest son of Raúl Castro is a high-ranking officer of the intelligence. Raúl´s son-in-law decides which enterprise receives permission to invest on the Island. Traditionally, the Castros attach great importance to their own security. The chief of Raúl Castro´s bodyguards is his grandson. Raúl´s daughter – MARIELA – runs a center for sexuality. Apparently it is an irrelevant position. In reality – MARIELA – acts as the main spokesperson of the Cuban government towards the West. In America and Europe, she transmits a friendly image of the Cuban system, presenting it as a bulwark against sexual discrimination. Experts on Cuban affairs consider her as a potential member of a future collective in the Cuban government aimed towards reforming the Castrismus. When this moment arrives, MARIELA will have the support from another prominent member of the Castro Clan: MARCOS PORTAL LEÓN. He is a former Minister and member of the Politburo of the Communist party. MARCOS PORTAL is the husband of one of Fidel's and Raúl´s nieces. He was a pioneer in introducing reforms in the Cuban economy. PORTAL convinced Fidel to open the Island to foreign enterprises. MARCOS PORTAL fell in disgrace – not because of his idea to introduce market-economy mechanisms in Cuba – but rather his bold step to designate my old friend – FIDELITO – as his personal adviser. In the 1980s, a handful of Cuban intelligence officers were punished by Fidel because they advocated reforms for the Cuban system. Castro interpreted this as an attempt to overthrow him from power. PORTAL recruited several of these officers to work with him. This also infuriated Fidel.

MARCOS PORTAL is smart and competent. Many Cuban experts target HIM as a possible key person in a future reform process. Aside having no more an official position, PORTAL maintains contacts with high-ranking members of the government.

The Castro Clan has been weakened after the illness of their leading figure. When FIDEL CASTRO was in full-health, the Clan was in harmony. In those days the Castros were a great family, similar to the Corleones of Mario Puzzo's novel. The absence of Fidel deepens the divisions between the two branches of the Clan: FIDEL´s family and RAUL´s family. The main person in Fidel´s family is his second wife DELIA SOTO. She and Fidel have four children together. The other branch of the Clan is Raúl Castro and his children with Vilma Espin, a former member of Castro´s guerrilla of the 1950s. For several decades, ESPIN was the First Lady of Cuba, not DELIA SOTO, the wife of Fidel Castro. This insignificant fact secretly disturbs relations between both branches of the Castro Clan, especially in the last few years. Raúl's children are more prominent than Fidel´s children. The most remarkable of Fidel´s children is his son ANTONIO, a doctor, who advises the Cuban government in medicine and sport. Alone – without their mother's support – they will not be able to have a major role in a future reform process. In the case of his mother DELIA SOTO, things could be different, because she is the real queen. The first time Cubans saw DELIA was alongside FIDEL CASTRO as his companion, when he handed over his power to his brother. Since then, in every public appearance, FIDEL CASTRO has DELIA by his side. Why does somebody who was quite unknown before, appear suddenly on the front pages of Cuban newspapers? Is this an attempt to position DELIA as the head of a movement of hardline communists defending the heritage of the Castrismus? As we know in the case of communist China, MAO´s wife Jiang Qing was a failure in the 1970s when she tried to seize power. If we want to talk about possible scenarios in Cuba, we should consider the possible role of DELIA.

Another interesting point is the controversial role of the Castro Clan in the Cuban public opinion. Recently, the Cuban newspaper Havana Tribune wrote a piece criticizing the luxurious lifestyle of FIDEL´s and DELIA´s youngest son. The most remarkable aspect was not the piece itself, but the fact

that neither the journalist, nor the director of the newspaper was punished. In Cuba, nobody dares to offend a member of the tropical “royal family”. That means there is somebody powerful enough to challenge the Clan, whose members are considered untouchable in Cuba. For me, two things are clear:
First: In the highest level of power, not everybody agrees with the idea of the Castro Clan remaining in power. Second: If criticism of the Castro family is suddenly allowed, this could mean the pyramid of power in Cuba is splitting and the future role of the Castro Clan is uncertain.

What is the recommended attitude, Europe and the United States should take towards the Castro Clan?

It would be a mistake to underestimate their role in the future, but it would also be naïve to deal with them as friends. The reforms that they are willing to accept do not contemplate changes of the magnitude that we have seen in China or other totalitarian regimes. They are not interested in improving the lives of the population. Their objective is to reach the point in that gathering riches ceases to be a political and legal crime. They wish to change this key point of the Castro doctrine in order to freely enjoy the millions they have illegally amassed in Cuba the last few years. They want economic freedom but only enough that allows them – under the current status quo—to maintain their perks. Human and political rights are not part of the Castro agenda.

MARIELA CASTRO travels to Western countries every year. I suggest paying more attention to her public appearances in order to know more about the trends and secret intentions of the Castro Clan.

Moving on to other issues, I invite you to evaluate my project RADIO CUBA DIALOGA. My idea is to broadcast a radio program to Cuba, inviting the audience to a sober analysis of their problems. RADIO CUBA DIALOGA encourages diversity of viewpoints and the building of bridges between juxtaposed positions.

The Castros belong to the past;

Radio Cuba Dialoga is a window to the future.

Boris Luis Santa Coloma:
El Clan de los Castro: Un obstáculo para un proceso de reformas cubano

Recuerdo el día en que conocí al hijo mayor de Fidel Castro. Fue en el año 1962. Lo trajo a mi casa un compañero de lucha de mi padre. Me llamó la atención por su manera desenvuelta, propia de quien está habituado a ser centro de atención. Le mostré unos comics americanos y muy serio me recomendó botar esa basura del imperialismo. Por aquel entonces nadie podía imaginar, que con el paso de los años, aquel joven antimperialista acabaría convirtiéndose en uno de los principales defensores de una apertura cubana a los grandes consorcios estadounidenses. El mayor de los hijos de Fidel heredó la inteligencia de su padre, no así su desconfianza hacia todos quienes le rodeaban, incluyendo su propia familia. Fidelito creció bajo la tutela de su tío Raúl y la atención personal de José Abrahantes, el jefe de los guardaespaldas del jefe de estado cubano. Todo parecía indicar que ocuparía un puesto relevante en las estructuras de poder, hasta que Fidel condenó a prisión al jefe de sus guardaespaldas, a quien acusó de simpatizar con la perestroika de Gorbachov. Fidelito salió en defensa de su tutor, la única persona en su niñez que siempre estaba a su lado, mientras Castro se dedicaba a hacer revoluciones por el mundo. Fidel castigó a su hijo por la ofensa de atreverse a cuestionar su decisión. Desde entonces Fidel Junior ha venido girando en la órbita próxima a su tío Raúl. Hoy le asesora en cuestiones internacionales, aprovechando su vasta experiencia especialmente en asuntos europeos.

A través de una red de empresas fantasmas – manejadas por extranjeros – el clan de los Castro ha amasado una fortuna cuya cuantía se desconoce. Pero su fuerza no emana de su poder económico, sino de su posicionamiento estratégico en las estructuras de poder y de su condición natural como baluartes de la continuidad del castrismo. La familia de los Castro controla ámbitos estratégicos del sistema gubernamental cubano. El hijo del presidente Raúl Castro es un alto oficial del espionaje cubano. Su yerno es quien da el visto bueno a las empresas extranjeras cuando solicitan hacer negocios con la Isla. Consciente del valor del espionaje y la seguridad para el éxito, el presidente Raúl Castro nombró a su nieto jefe de sus guardaespaldas. Su hija –

MARIELA - dirige un centro de estudios sobre sexualidad. Aparentemente una función irrelevante. Sin embargo es ella el principal portavoz ideológico del castrismo, divulgando en el extranjero una faz amable de la dictadura cubana, presentándola como un baluarte de la libertad sexual en el mundo. Expertos en la materia ven a Mariela como parte de una futura dirección colegiada, que sería la encargada de administrar el patrimonio ideológico del castrismo, pero sin los prejuicios de Fidel Castro quien consideraba la acumulación de riquezas como una aberración. Cuando llegue ese momento de la transición, MARIELA contará con la importantísima ayuda de otro miembro del clan, MARCOS PORTAL LEÓN, un ex ministro casado con una sobrina de Fidel y Raúl, quien fue el precursor del proceso de apertura de Cuba a las empresas extranjeras, pues fue el primero del gobierno cubano que logró convencer a Fidel para que abriese el país a las empresas extranjeras. Al final Fidel le castigó, no tanto por su osadía de introducir mecanismos de economía de mercado, sino por designar como su asesor personal a Fidelito y a otros caídos en desgracia, especialmente ex oficiales de los servicios secretos, castigados por Castro por coquetear abiertamente con la idea de una reforma del sistema cubano.

El clan se ha debilitado por la ausencia de su máxima figura, el gran patriarca, atenazado por la demencia, las enfermedades y los años. Cuando Fidel Castro se encontraba en plenitud de sus facultades, reinaba armonía familiar. Los Castro eran una gran familia, semejante a los Corleone. Pero con el ocaso del patriarca, comenzaron a aflorar diferencias. De un lado está la rama familiar encabezada por Delia Soto, la segunda mujer de Fidel Castro, con quien el ex guerrillero generó cuatro hijos. Del otro está Raúl Castro y sus hijos generados con Vilma Espín, un líder histórico de la guerrilla castrista, ya fallecida y que fue durante décadas la primera dama de la república. Castro, al igual que Hitler y Stalin, guardaba en el mayor secreto la existencia de su familia. De ahí que la elegida para ser la primera dama del país no fue su esposa legítima, sino su cuñada. Este hecho sin embargo creó un mal de fondo, que ha enturbiado las secretas relaciones entre ambas ramas del clan, especialmente en los últimos años. A diferencia de los hijos de Raúl Castro, los de Fidel y Delia Soto no son sobresalientes. El más notable es

Antonio, un médico, que actualmente asesora al gobierno cubano en temas médicos y deportivos. Considero poco probable que los hijos de Fidel y Delia puedan por sí solos – sin la ayuda materna - desempeñar un papel relevante en un futuro. Otra cosa es su madre, Delia, la reina legítima. Cuando la enfermedad obligó a Fidel a dejar el poder, los cubanos vieron por primera vez a Delia. Desde entonces ella no falta en cada aparición pública del patriarca. ¿Por qué esa decisión de sacar a la palestra pública a alguien hasta la fecha desconocido? ¿Existe algún testamento político secreto? Se sabe que Stalin cambió el testamento de Lenin con la ayuda de su mujer, pero Stalin era una figura política. ¿Estaría Delia dispuesta a encabezar un movimiento de la rama ortodoxa del castrismo, en el caso de una rebelión girondina en defensa de los principios fidelistas? En China la mujer de Mao, YAN KIN, lo intentó tras la muerte del Gran Timonel y fracasó. Si vamos a hablar sobre escenarios futuros, no podemos descartar el papel, que podría eventualmente desempeñar esta mujer en el proceso de cambios profundos que seguramente deberá tener lugar en Cuba próximamente.

El papel del clan es controvertido en la opinión pública cubana. Hace unas semanas el diario Tribuna de La Habana publicó un artículo criticando el modo de vida del hijo menor de Fidel y Delia Soto, cuyos viajes de placer constituyen un escándalo en un país plagado por la pobreza. El articulo – titulado "Los Viajes de Gulliver" – estaba escrito en ese lenguaje críptico propio de la prensa de países comunistas cuando quiere criticar a alguien o algo vinculado con las altas esferas del poder. Lo notable del incidente no es solo la publicación del artículo en sí, sino el hecho de que ni el autor ni la directora del diario fueron castigados. Nadie por iniciativa propia se atrevería a criticar en público a la familia real sin contar con la protección debida. El inspirador fue alguien seguramente con poder suficiente como para desafiar las iras de la familia Castro. Ello indica dos cosas: Que el clan Castro no las tiene todas consigo y que existen tendencias no convergentes entre las altas esferas del poder en Cuba en cuanto al papel futuro de la dinastía.

¿Qué actitud deben asumir Europa y Estados Unidos hacia la familia Castro?

Sería un error subestimar un león hambriento de poder, de la misma manera que sería ingenuo considerarlo un amigo. Los Castros quieren una reforma profunda de la economía cubana, pero solo porque la consideran el único camino viable para mantener el sistema totalitario actual. Su convicción sobre la necesidad de reformas emana de su instinto de supervivencia, no de una convicción sobre el fracaso del sistema económico impuesto por Castro. Tal vez crean por eso que la opción indicada sea algo semejante a lo que hay en China o Vietnam. Ni las libertades individuales ni la democracia parecen importarles mucho. La cabeza visible del clan, Mariela Castro, viaja mucho por Occidente. Tal vez sería prudente evaluar con un poco más de detenimiento sus declaraciones públicas y así descubrir las verdaderas secretas intenciones del Clan de los Castro.

Propongo a los presentes evaluar mi proyecto Radio Cuba Dialoga como una respuesta indicada e innovadora para contribuir a que los cubanos tomen el destino en sus manos al margen de las intenciones de una dinastía que desgobierna Cuba desde hace más de medio siglo. Radio Cuba Dialoga es un proyecto para promover un diálogo entre cubanos, aprovechando la oportunidad que brindan las estaciones de radio que transmiten desde los cayos de la Florida y que pueden ser captadas en el occidente y el centro de Cuba.

Los Castro son el pasado,
Radio Cuba Dialoga es una ventana al futuro.

¡Les doy las gracias por su atención!

Part 3: Lessons learnt from 1989/90

Reinhard Weißhuhn:
Human rights in the German Democratic Republic and Hungary

Since the beginning of de-Stalinization in the Soviet Union in 1956, the Eastern bloc countries began to develop in different ways. The corset of Stalinism loosened and the scope for the individual governor of the Soviet Union grew. However, this did not mean that the Stalinist system of despotism had been abolished. It also did not mean that opinions, which differed from the Stalinist dogma or its interpretation by the rulers, were tolerated. But it meant that different degrees of consequences of the repression could emerge in the individual countries.

These differences were naturally based on the different historical developments and backgrounds. In the GDR, for example, there was practically no de-Stalinization. It was slowly admitted that there had been some problems earlier, and they were consistently related to the exaggerated cult of personality around Stalin. Otherwise, little changed, and certainly not more than in the Soviet Union itself. The recurrent genocidal purges and waves of arrests had already ended with Stalin's death in 1953. The brutal terror had given way to more subtle forms of oppression.

After the military abolition of the national uprising in the GDR in 1953, every oppositional impulse was gone for a long time. Who was unhappy, fled to the West. This option was impossible with the construction of the Wall in 1961. Until then, millions had already turned their backs on the GDR. Among these were also the remnants of the bourgeois classes and liberal intellectuals, who had survived the Third Reich and the era of Stalin. The Society of the GDR was successfully destroyed. Oppositional seeds had to first re-develop, for which it took new generations. The first of these generations was banished out of the country, back in the late 70's - the keyword for this is the expatriation of Wolf Biermann in 1976. This generation was explicitly left-wing. Their criticism of the GDR combined them with an equivalent critique of capitalism that is the other German state.

However, 1976 is very important regarding another aspect of the developments in the GDR. In Helsinki, the governments of all states of the Warsaw Pact and the West signed the Final Act of the CSCE and therefore their "3rd basket". This act bounds all states to respect human rights. The GDR as all other states of the Eastern Bloc saw themselves forced to accept it in order to not jeopardize its growing economic dependence on trade with the West. Another reason for the GDR was as well the fact that they were still fighting for its international recognition. This has indeed already been done in 1973 with the inclusion in the UN, but the old inferiority complex of the ruling had not yet been overcome.

Of course, the ruling Communists in all countries of the Eastern Bloc did not think for a second to obey the obligations of Helsinki. This, they knew, would have been the end of their rule. Inwardly they foiled, at least in the German Democratic Republic, the human rights with ever tighter political penal laws. Because they also knew that they had created a possibility for attacks by signing the Final Act, a court of appeal for those who wanted to claim their human rights. This was one of the aids in the development of a second generation of oppositionists from the late 70s, which were no longer traditional left, but were oriented towards democracy and human rights. From the left and the Christian seeds of this second generation a hard core of oppositionists arose from the second half of the 70s. For the first time in the history of the GDR, a substantive and personal continuity of opposition could emerge, which was more than just a shooting star with the live span of just a few years. This hard core succeeded finally in 1989 to mobilize a mass movement that abolished the rule of the Communists in a peaceful revolution.

The despotism remained in the GDR until its end; there were no political rights, no freedom of travel and of course no rule of law. If there was still the opportunity for growth of an opposition, then it was not because of a conscious-driven liberalization, but rather because of the erosion of the state and its ever-growing dependence on the West. But all opposition activities stayed illegal and were threatened with drastic punishments. At least outside the province, however, these activities were pursued increasingly rare with reasonable consistency. There have been repeated arrests and interrogations, house inspections, apartment withdrawals, study bans etc., plus a massive penetration by the secret police. But the bigger and bolder the opposition got, the more known it was in the population, the better it was interconnected, the more contacts in the West and in the communist neighbor countries it had, the harder it was for the rulers to handle this dynamic.

Next to the Czechoslovakian Charter 77 and the Polish Solidarność was the democratic opposition in Hungary one of the models for the opposition in the GDR. The Hungarian opposition consisted of a larger group of conservative nationalists and a small group of liberals, oriented to democracy and human rights, which was practically limited to the capital Budapest. They emerged - like in the GDR - from neo-Marxist roots in the 70s. In the 80s, they could, although illegal, largely undisturbed by the state, run publishing houses, publish magazines and even teach at universities. This was a result of conscious political and economic liberalization.

After the military abolition of the Hungarian revolution in 1956, the Stalinist regime had been replaced by a group of Communists, which were pursuing pragmatic power politics. They acted politically more undogmatic and more technocratic in the economy than their neighbors in the Soviet bloc. This is how, over the time the image of Hungary as the "funniest barrack in the camp" developed. Still, in the second half of the 60s the liberalization remained fragile and arbitrary. Also in Hungary, there was neither democracy nor the rule of law. But twenty years of development had given enough space for niches of free development, to enable a relatively diverse intellectual and cultural landscape.

The Hungarian Communists also recognized earlier than their comrades elsewhere, that the end of their rule was approaching. Not coincidentally, the Iron Curtain was first opened in Hungary. The democratic opposition played an important political role in the first years after the fall of communism. Meanwhile, the conservative nationalist majority has prevailed and the Hungarian government proclaimed to the applause of their electorate an explicitly "illiberal" state. Unfortunately, democracy is no guarantee of progress...

Reinhard Weißhuhn: Menschenrechte in der DDR und in Ungarn

Seit dem Beginn der Entstalinisierung in der Sowjetunion 1956 begannen die Staaten des Ostblocks sich langsam unterschiedlicher zu entwickeln. Das Korsett des Stalinismus lockerte sich, der Spielraum für die einzelnen Statthalter der Sowjetunion wuchs. Das bedeutete jedoch nicht, dass das stalinistische System von Willkür aufgehoben worden wäre. Es bedeutete auch nicht, dass von nun an Meinungen geduldet worden wären, die vom stalinistischen Dogma oder seiner Interpretation durch die Herrschenden abwichen. Aber es bedeutete, dass sich in den einzelnen Ländern unterschiedliche Grade an Konsequenz der Unterdrückung herausbilden konnten.

Diese Unterschiede hatten natürlich mit unterschiedlichen historischen Entwicklungen und Hintergründen zu tun. In der DDR zum Beispiel gab es praktisch keine Entstalinisierung. Zögernd wurde zugestanden, dass es früher gewisse Probleme gegeben habe, und diese hätten durchweg mit dem übertriebenen Personenkult um Stalin zu tun.

Ansonsten änderte sich wenig, und schon gar nicht mehr als in der Sowjetunion selbst. Die wiederkehrenden massenmörderischen Säuberungen und Verhaftungswellen waren schon mit Stalins Tod 1953 beendet worden. Der brutale Terror war subtileren Formen der Unterdrückung gewichen.

Nach der militärischen Niederschlagung des Volksaufstands in der DDR 1953 war für lange Zeit jede oppositionelle Regung erstickt. Wer unzufrieden war, floh in den Westen. Das wurde mit dem Bau der Mauer 1961 unmöglich. Bis dahin hatten bereits Millionen der DDR den Rücken gekehrt. Zu diesen gehörten auch jene Reste bürgerlicher Schichten und liberaler Intellektueller, die das Dritte Reich und die Stalin-Zeit überlebt hatten. Die Gesellschaft der DDR war erfolgreich zerstört. Oppositionelle Keime mussten sich erst wieder neu entwickeln, und dazu bedurfte es neuer Generationen. Die erste dieser Generationen wurde bereits in den späten 70er Jahren außer Landes getrieben - das Stichwort hierzu ist die Ausbürgerung von Wolf Biermann 1976. Diese Generation war eine explizit linke. Ihre Kritik an der DDR verband sie mit gleichwertiger Kritik am Kapitalismus, also am anderen deutschen Staat.

Das Jahr 1976 ist aber in einer weiteren Hinsicht wichtig für die Entwicklung in der DDR. In Helsinki unterzeichneten die Regierungen aller Staaten des Warschauer Paktes und des Westens die Schlußakte der KSZE und damit ihres "Korbs III". Dieser verpflichtete alle Staaten zur Einhaltung der Menschenrechte. Die DDR wie alle anderen Staaten des Ostblocks sahen sich zu diesem Zugeständnis genötigt, um ihre wachsende wirtschaftliche Abhängigkeit vom Handel mit dem Westen nicht zu gefährden. Für die DDR kam hinzu, dass sie noch immer um ihre internationale Anerkennung kämpfte. Diese war zwar bereits 1973 mit der Aufnahme in die UN erfolgt, aber der alte Minderwertigkeitskomplex der Herrschenden war noch nicht überwunden.

Die herrschenden Kommunisten in allen Ländern des Ostblocks dachten natürlich keine Sekunde daran, die Verpflichtung von Helsinki ernst zu nehmen und umzusetzen. Das, so wußten sie, wäre das Ende ihrer Herrschaft gewesen. Nach innen konterkarierten sie, jedenfalls in der DDR, die Menschenrechte schon prophylaktisch mit immer schärferen politischen Strafgesetzen. Denn sie wußten auch, dass sie mit der Unterzeichnung der Schlußakte eine Angriffsfläche geschaffen hatten, eine Berufungsinstanz für jene, die ihre Menschenrechte beanspruchen wollten. Dies war eine der Hilfen bei der Entwicklung einer zweiten Generation von Oppositionellen ab Ende der 70er Jahre, die nicht mehr traditionell links, sondern an Demokratie und Menschenrechten orientiert war. Aus den linken und den christlichen Keimen dieser zweiten Generation entstand seit der zweiten Hälfte der 70er Jahre ein harter Kern von Oppositionellen. Zum ersten Mal in der Geschichte der DDR konnte sich eine inhaltliche und personelle Kontinuität von Opposition herausbilden, die mehr als nur eine Sternschnuppe von wenigen Jahren Lebensdauer war. Diesem harten Kern gelang es schließlich 1989 eine Massenbewegung zu mobilisieren, die in der friedlichen Revolution die Herrschaft der Kommunisten beseitigte.

Die staatliche Willkür blieb der DDR bis zu ihrem Ende erhalten, es gab keinerlei politische Rechte, keine Reisefreiheit und natürlich keinen Rechtsstaat. Wenn dennoch eine Opposition wachsen konnte, so lag das nicht an einer bewußt betriebenen Liberalisierung, sondern an der Erosion des Staates und seiner immer weiter wachsenden Abhängigkeit vom Westen. Zwar blieben alle oppositionellen

Aktivitäten illegal und waren mit drastischen Strafen bedroht. Zumindest außerhalb der Provinz jedoch wurden diese Aktivitäten immer seltener mit hinreichender Konsequenz verfolgt. Es gab immer wieder Festnahmen und Verhöre, Haussuchungen, Berufsverbote, Wohnungsentzug, Studiumsverbot usw., dazu eine massive Durchdringung durch die Geheimpolizei. Aber je größer und mutiger die Opposition wurde, je bekannter sie in der Bevölkerung wurde, je besser sie vernetzt war, je mehr Kontakte sie in den Westen und in die kommunistischen Nachbarländer knüpfen konnte, desto schwieriger wurde es für die Herrschenden, dieser Dynamik noch Herr zu werden.

Neben der tschechoslowakischen Charta 77 und der polnischen Solidarność war die demokratische Opposition in Ungarn eines der Vorbilder für die Oppositionellen in der DDR. Die ungarische Opposition bestand aus einer größeren Gruppe von konservativen Nationalisten und einer kleinen liberalen, an Demokratie und Menschenrechten orientierten Gruppe, die praktisch auf die Hauptstadt Budapest beschränkt war. Entstanden war diese - ähnlich wie in der DDR - aus neomarxistischen Wurzeln in den 70er Jahren. In den 80er Jahren konnte sie, wenngleich illegal, weitgehend unbehelligt vom Staat Verlage betreiben, Zeitschriften herausgeben und sogar an Universitäten lehren. Dies war eine Folge bewußter politischer und wirtschaftlicher Liberalisierung.

Nach der militärischen Niederschlagung der ungarischen Revolution von 1956 war das stalinistische Regime durch eine Gruppe von Kommunisten ersetzt worden, die pragmatische Machtpolitik betrieb. Sie agierte politisch undogmatischer und in der Wirtschaft technokratischer als ihre Nachbarn im Ostblock. So entstand im Laufe der Zeit das Image Ungarns als der "lustigsten Baracke im Lager". Zwar blieb auch diese in der zweiten Hälfte der 60er Jahre einsetzende Liberalisierung fragil und willkürlich. Auch in Ungarn gab es weder Demokratie noch Rechtsstaat. Aber zwanzig Jahre Entwicklung hatten genügend Nischen freier Entfaltung entstehen lassen, um eine relativ vielfältige intellektuelle und kulturelle Landschaft zu ermöglichen.

Die ungarischen Kommunisten erkannten auch früher als ihre Genossen woanders, dass das Ende ihrer Herrschaft nahte. Nicht zufällig wurde zuerst in Ungarn der Eiserne Vorhang geöffnet. Die demokratische Opposition spielte in den ersten Jahren nach dem Ende des Kommunismus eine wichtige politische Rolle. Inzwischen hat sich die konservativ-nationalistische Mehrheit durchgesetzt und die ungarische Regierung proklamiert unter dem Beifall ihrer Wählerschaft einen explizit "illiberalen" Staat. Demokratie ist leider auch keine Garantie für Fortschritt...

Part 4:

The Cuba Strategy from a German perspective

Markus Meckel:

Cuba strategy: Design for a social democratic position determination

Social Democrats for a self-determined development of Cuba

We Social Democrats support a new policy in and for Cuba, which is committed to a self-determined and democratic future for the Cuban people.

We Social Democrats condemn dictatorship and oppression, injustice and lack of freedom all over the world. We foster a culture of dialogue and balance of interests. This can defuse conflicts and ensure sustainable, peaceful coexistence.

We Social Democrats are placing an emphasis also towards Cuba on cooperation rather than confrontation, on dialogue rather than isolation. Only then we can call our own values openly and convince others of them.

Cuba today

To date, the Cuban governance understood itself as the bearer of the revolution ideals, although it has departed from freedom and social justice long ago. Even if the revolution 50 years ago overthrew the US-backed regime of Fulgencio Batista and therefore brought the chance for freedom to the Cuban people, so Cuba has developed to a Communist dictatorship under the decades-long reign of Fidel Castro and significantly influenced by the global political conditions of the Cold War. So, the talk of revolution was more and more becoming an ideology of legitimation for a repressive, communist oriented, system. Through the dual monetary system and through targeted Alimentation by friendly States, particularly from Latin America, the survival of the population is indeed guaranteed; nevertheless, the economic infrastructure of the country is in a largely dilapidated condition and providing the population with food is not assured in many places. The same applies to the former achievements in education and health, which are, for the availability of resources, further away from the former glory than ever.

After Fidel Castro withdrew from all official posts in early 2008, his brother Raúl took over the affairs of state. Cuba today has the chance to initiate the transition to greater freedom, democracy and prosperity. The Cubans are hoping that the new government will improve their material situation and more opportunities for private initiatives, but above all political freedom and civil liberties. First signals in both directions have been sent with the recent decisions to facilitate the purchase of electronic communications equipment, the enabled smallholders' access to land, seed and fertilizer, as well as initiated public debates from the party and government in the state of the economy and society. The implementation of these initiatives will prove whether the participation of the population remains not only as a fig leaf, but the beginning of a new future.

On the situation of political freedoms and human rights

The political liberties such as freedom of expression, association and assembly remain severely limited to date under Raúl Castro. The control of the population by the Cuban intelligence leads to progressive disillusionment and loss of confidence in broad sections of the population. In addition to the largely effective social control, there remain often abnormal operations of the police and military.

Nevertheless, with the “International Covenant on Civil and Political Rights” and the “International Covenant on

Economic, Social and Cultural Rights", Cuba has signed the two basic human rights covenants of the United Nations on 28 February 2008. But only with the pending ratification of both covenants and by national legal and factual implementation, the outspoken commitment to human rights will gain credibility.

With the release of political prisoners and an expanded scope of the Catholic Church, Cuba has sent welcome signals. At the same time, however, still many dissidents are in prison, many of them are ill due to mostly poor conditions. Fast ensuring emergency medical treatment as well as the release of all political prisoners remains our urgent demands. The families of the political prisoners, the "Ladies in White" (Las Damas de Blanco) have our solidarity!

The developments mentioned under Raúl Castro, however, should be taken seriously as the first steps of an open process. We call on the Cuban government and the Communist Party of Cuba, to continuously pursue the process of opening and to in fact observe the commitments made by signing the two human rights covenants. We offer to initiate a human rights dialogue as one that has been established with the PRC for many years.

Cautious signs of economic openness

Since the government takeover by Raúl Castro, Cuba is economically in a cautious reform process. As a longtime defense minister, Raul Castro had access to significant parts of the Cuban economy. With the help of the military, which manages the strategic areas in the form of state-owned enterprises itself, he is now trying to control the identified necessary economic opening process. Raúl Castro was always firmly anchored in the Communist Party and was from this position able to initiate some economic reforms out in the 1990s.

Cuba faces the enormous challenge of building an efficient economy, to ensure a stable supply of the population with food and household goods. The transport infrastructure is dilapidated; reorganization is especially in the sugar cane sector urgently needed. In particular in the fields of tourism and bioethanol production, great potential remains untapped due to the inflexible central state planning economy.

With its recently announced approaches of economic reforms, Raúl Castro wants to make government work more efficiently and boost the agricultural production important for the supply of the population. This is intended to encourage small farmers and small private companies. Cautious incentives and reduced bureaucratic requirements shall motivate the Cubans to become self-employed. Nonetheless, the now ongoing reforms are primarily serving the system stabilization. It remains unclear, how certain the lastly allotted plots to smallholders will remain with them. The transmission of reliable legal and property titles is central.

A three-pronged strategy for democratic change in Cuba

The EU has started to make the relationship with Cuba new and differentiated. After freezing of the political and cultural cooperation between Cuba and the EU in the wake of the convictions of political prisoners in 2003, an attempt for a new beginning is made. Cuba now also accepts the EU offer of a constructive and inclusive political dialogue.

A policy of small steps and permanent dialogue is promising under the current conditions. As in Detente-times in the

East-West conflict, a model of gradual approach should be reflected also in the relations with Cuba: Not a fundamental willingness to engage in dialogue, but rather the content of negotiations and progress should be linked to concrete conditions.

Here, a twofold dialogue approach is required: Maintaining of conversation contacts with the Cuban government and at the same time solidarity and support for civil society and the peaceful democratic opposition.

Especially in the current phase of a leadership transition, it is important to maintain conversations with the government and the Communist Party at all levels, thus getting to know the next generation of leaders and to back up the reform willing. The party and state should not be understood as a monolithic block.

Democratic change cannot be created from the outside; it has to develop in Cuba itself and from its population. The support of civic engagement and its institutions, the development of free and uncensored media and democratic political movements is central to the development of a broad social basis for democratic change and a self-determined of the Cuban people.

In Cuba, a number of hopeful initiatives have developed, which occur at high risk and with great commitment to democratic change. They need to be supported and with them a continuous dialogue should be maintained. These include the political projects "Varela" and "Todos Cubanos" by Oswaldo Payá Sardiñas, the social projects for women of "FLAMUR" and the educational projects of the Catholic Church, such as the "Association of Independent Libraries".

Given the cautious economic reforms the double dialogue approach should be complemented by a third, independent emphasized dimension, which can respond to opening signals on the Cuban side and at the same time act as a hinge between the two other target areas - governance and society: To improve the economic situation and in particular the supply of the population, the economic cooperation with Cuba should be strengthened. An increase in development resources and targeted encouragement to FDI should however be implemented gradually. In appropriate steps, Cuba should simultaneously accept the formation of free trade unions, guarantee the payment of fair wages and secure respect for central workers' rights.

The embargo for Cuba imposed by the United States, particularly its intensification by the Helms-Burton Act in 1996, have proven in recent years to be counterproductive. Given the characters of cautious opening in Cuba, the US should just now be encouraged to give up its blockade policy - and in particular, the companies from third countries affecting tightening - and join the dialogue and cooperation strategy described. A pragmatic course of the USA towards Cuba can help to create trade, which directly benefits the economic structure and the population of Cuba. The timing for such a reorientation of policy towards Cuba is with the change of administration in the United States today much cheaper than ever before.

Ways and means of support of democratic change in Cuba

On all three levels - in the political dialogue at all levels of government, in dialogue with and in support of civil society and the democratic opposition, in the field of economic cooperation - concrete projects should gradually be agreed and implemented. With advances, their expansion should be monitored continuously.

With the presence and the expansion of the work of political foundations in Cuba, a partnership and constructive dialogue on the political and social challenges of our time can be started. In particular, in the development of a pluralistic press and media system, with regard to the preparation and execution of democratic elections and to create awareness of workers' rights, our political foundations can provide theoretical and practical knowledge, launch discussions and help to gather the relevant actors. The SPD should also take the initiative and suggest that the Socialist Internationals send an exploratory commission to Cuba to check if and when a status can be granted to the Social Democratic Party of Cuba (chaired by Vladimiro Roca Antúnez) and the Socialist Party “Arco Progresista” (chaired by Manuel Cuesta Morúa).

With the conclusion of a cultural agreement and the early opening of a Goethe Institute, the political dialogue on the cultural level can be extended and deepened. By once very close relations with the GDR, many Cubans have good knowledge of the German language, to which the establishment of a German school or a reinforced range of German lessons can be attached. Equally important are the intensification of scientific exchange, the demand for a resumption of fair and transparent awarding of state grants and the resumption of a bilateral economic and technological cooperation.

In connection with the social and economic transformation process, projects should be developed for reforming the current system of dual currencies, for the reform of the judicial and administrative nature, for the conversion of social security to a system of negative income tax, for the development of agriculture and favor improving economic productivity and sustainability in general. Of great urgency are also fundamental issues of justice of distribution and performance.

Acute assistance in coping with the damage repeatedly caused by tropical storms should be offered as short-term and unbureaucratic.

Numerous contacts at a civil society level should be encouraged and expanded. These include municipal partnerships and those between unions, associations and cultural institutions. Also the contacts of the churches in the context of community partnerships, the ecumenical exchanges, in diaconal and educational work should be strengthened.

Seize opportunities now!

Cuba is in a transitional phase. Raúl Castro seems to herald a cautious policy change. Although it is still open at this point of time, one doesn't know where this process will lead. However, chances of development are opened towards democracy and the rule of law. We expect further significant steps to open up and democratize the country, we want to contribute to a clear and coherent EU policy towards Cuba and assist Cubans in shaping their future development path.

By Markus Meckel, MP | Effective: December 2008

Markus Meckel:
Kuba-Strategie: Entwurf für eine sozialdemokratische Positionsbestimmung

Sozialdemokraten für eine selbstbestimmte Entwicklung Kubas

Wir Sozialdemokraten unterstützen eine neue Politik auf und für Kuba, welche sich für eine selbstbestimmte und demokratische Zukunft des kubanischen Volkes einsetzt.

Wir Sozialdemokraten verurteilen überall in der Welt Diktatur und Unterdrückung, Ungerechtigkeit und Unfreiheit. Wir pflegen eine Kultur des Dialogs und des Ausgleichs der Interessen. Dies kann Konflikte entschärfen und friedliches Zusammenleben nachhaltig sichern.

Wir Sozialdemokraten setzen auch gegenüber Kuba auf Kooperation statt Konfrontation, auf Dialog statt Isolation. Nur so können wir unsere eigenen Werte offen benennen und andere von ihnen überzeugen.

Kuba heute

Bis heute versteht sich die kubanische Staatsführung als Trägerin der Revolutionsideale, obgleich sie sich bereits vor langer Zeit von den einstigen Grundsätzen Freiheit und sozialer Gerechtigkeit verabschiedet hat. Wenn auch die Revolution vor 50 Jahren das von den USA gestützte Regime Fulgencio Batistas stürzte und damit dem kubanischen Volk die Chance zur Freiheit brachte, so hat sich Kuba unter der jahrzehntelangen Regierungszeit Fidel Castros und maßgeblich beeinflusst durch die globalpolitischen Bedingungen des Kalten Krieges zu einer kommunistischen Diktatur entwickelt. So wurde die Rede von der Revolution immer mehr zu einer Legitimationsideologie für ein repressives, an kommunistischen Vorbildern ausgerichtetes System. Durch das duale Währungssystem und mittels gezielter Alimentation durch befreundete Staaten insbesondere aus Lateinamerika wird das Überleben der Bevölkerung zwar gewährleistet; dennoch befindet sich die wirtschaftliche Infrastruktur des Landes in einem weitgehend maroden Zustand und die Versorgung der Bevölkerung mit Nahrungsmitteln ist vielerorts nicht sichergestellt. Ähnliches gilt für die einstigen

Errungenschaften im Bildungs- und Gesundheitswesen, welche beide aufgrund mangelnder Ressourcen vom Vorbildglanz alter Tage weiter denn je entfernt sind.

Nachdem sich Fidel Castro Anfang 2008 von allen offiziellen Ämtern zurückzog, übernahm sein Bruder Raúl die Regierungsgeschäfte. Kuba hat damit heute die Chance, den Wandel zu mehr Freiheit, Demokratie und Wohlstand einzuleiten. Die KubanerInnen erhoffen sich von der neuen Regierung eine Verbesserung ihrer materiellen Lage und mehr Möglichkeiten zu privaten Initiativen, vor allem aber auch politische Freiräume und Freiheitsrechte. Erste Signale in beide Richtungen sind mit den letzten Entscheidungen zum erleichterten Kauf von elektronischen Kommunikationsgeräten, dem ermöglichten Zugang von Kleinbauern zu Ackerland, Saatgut und Dünger sowie mit der zuletzt von Partei und Regierung angestoßenen öffentlichen Debatte über den Zustand von Wirtschaft und Gesellschaft ausgesandt worden. An der Umsetzung dieser Initiativen wird sich erweisen, ob die Beteiligung der Bevölkerung nicht nur ein Feigenblatt bleibt, sondern den Aufbruch in eine neue Zukunft verheißt.

Zur Lage der politischen Freiheiten und der Menschenrechte

Die politischen Freiheitsrechte wie die Meinungs-, Vereinigungs- und Versammlungsfreiheit bleiben bislang auch unter Raúl Castro stark eingeschränkt. Die Kontrolle der Bevölkerung durch den kubanischen Geheimdienst führt zu fortschreitender Desillusionierung und Vertrauensverlust in breiten Bevölkerungsschichten. Neben der weitgehend wirksamen sozialen Kontrolle gibt es weiterhin die oft unverhältnismäßigen Einsätze von Polizei und Militär.

Dennoch hat Kuba am 28. Februar 2008 mit dem „Internationalen Pakt über Bürgerliche und Politische Rechte" sowie dem „Internationalen Pakt über Wirtschaftliche, Soziale und Kulturelle Rechte" die beiden grundlegenden Menschenrechtspakte der Vereinten Nationen unterzeichnet. Doch erst mit der noch ausstehenden Ratifikation beider Pakte sowie durch die innerstaatliche rechtliche und faktische Implementierung wird das damit ausgesprochene Bekenntnis zu den Menschenrechten Glaubwürdigkeit erlangen.

Mit der Freilassung politischer Gefangener und einem erweiterten Handlungsspielraum für die katholische Kirche hat Kuba begrüßenswerte Signale gesendet. Gleichzeitig jedoch befinden sich noch immer viele Dissidenten in Haft, viele von ihnen sind ob der zumeist schlechten Haftbedingungen erkrankt. Die schnelle Gewährleistung dringend notwendiger medizinischer Behandlung sowie die Freilassung aller politischen Häftlinge bleiben unsere dringenden Forderungen. Die Familien der politischen Gefangenen, die „Damen in Weiß“ (Las Damas de Blanco) haben unsere Solidarität!

Die genannten Entwicklungen unter Raúl Castro sollten jedoch als erste Schritte eines Öffnungsprozesses ernst genommen werden. Wir fordern die kubanische Regierung und die Kommunistische Partei Kubas auf, den Prozess der Öffnung kontinuierlich fortzusetzen und die mit der Unterzeichnung der beiden Menschenrechtspakte eingegangenen Verpflichtungen auch tatsächlich einzuhalten. Wir bieten an, einen Menschenrechtsdialog zu initiieren, wie er auch mit der VR China bereits seit vielen Jahren etabliert ist.

Vorsichtige Zeichen der wirtschaftlichen Öffnung

Seit der Regierungsübernahme durch Raúl Castro befindet sich Kuba auch wirtschaftlich in einem vorsichtigen Reformprozess. Als langjähriger Verteidigungsminister hatte Raúl Castro Zugriff auf bedeutende Teile der kubanischen Wirtschaft. Mit Hilfe des Militärs, welches die strategischen Bereiche in Form von Staatsunternehmen selbst bewirtschaftet, versucht er nun, den als notwendig erkannten wirtschaftlichen Öffnungsprozess zu kontrollieren. Raúl Castro ist von jeher fest in der Kommunistischen Partei verankert und konnte aus dieser Position heraus in den 1990er Jahren einige Wirtschaftsreformen initiieren.

Kuba steht vor der enormen Herausforderung, eine effiziente Wirtschaft aufzubauen, um eine stabile Versorgung der Bevölkerung mit Nahrungsmitteln und Gebrauchsgütern zu gewährleisten. Die Transport-infrastruktur ist marode, eine Neuordnung vor allem des Zuckerrohrsektors dringend notwendig. Insbesondere in den Bereichen Tourismus und Bioethanolproduktion verbleibt aufgrund der unflexiblen zentralstaatlichen Planungswirtschaft großes Potential ungenutzt.

Mit seinen zuletzt angekündigten Ansätzen wirtschaftlicher Reformen will Raúl Castro die Arbeit der Regierung effizienter gestalten und die für die Versorgung der Bevölkerung wichtige landwirtschaftliche Produktion ankurbeln. Dadurch sollen Kleinbauern und kleine private Unternehmen gefördert werden. Vorsichtige Leistungsanreize und reduzierte bürokratische Vorgaben sollen die KubanerInnen motivieren, selbständig tätig zu werden. Nichtsdestotrotz dienen die jetzt begonnenen Reformen in erster Linie der Systemstabilisierung. Unklar bleibt überdies, wie sicher den Kleinbauern die ihnen zuletzt zugeteilten Parzellen erhalten bleiben. Zentral ist die Übertragung verlässlicher Rechts- und Besitztitel.

Eine dreigleisige Strategie für demokratischen Wandel auf Kuba

Die EU hat begonnen, das Verhältnis zu Kuba neu und differenzierter zu gestalten. Nach dem Einfrieren der politischen und kulturellen Zusammenarbeit zwischen Kuba und der EU in der Folge der Verurteilungen politischer

Häftlinge im Jahr 2003 wird nun der Versuch eines Neuanfangs gemacht. Kuba hat das EU-Angebot der Aufnahme eines konstruktiven und umfassenden politischen Dialogs nun auch angenommen.

Eine Politik der kleinen Schritte und des ständigen Dialogs ist unter den gegenwärtigen Bedingungen erfolgversprechend. Wie zu Detente-Zeiten im Ost-West-Konflikt sollte auch in den Beziehungen zu Kuba ein Modell der graduellen Annäherung zum Tragen kommen: Nicht die grundsätzliche Bereitschaft zum Dialog, sondern vielmehr die Verhandlungsinhalte und -fortschritte sollten an konkrete Bedingungen geknüpft werden.

Dabei ist ein doppelter Dialogansatz geboten: Unterhaltung von Gesprächskontakten mit der kubanischen Regierung bei gleichzeitiger Solidarität und Unterstützung für die Zivilgesellschaft und die friedliche demokratische Opposition.

Gerade in der aktuellen Phase eines Führungswechsels ist es wichtig, mit der Regierung und der Kommunistischen Partei auf allen Ebenen im Gespräch zu bleiben, somit die nächste Führungsgeneration kennenzulernen und den Reformwilligen den Rücken zu stärken. Partei und Staat dürfen nicht als monolithischer Block begriffen werden.

Demokratischer Wandel kann nicht von außen geschaffen werden, er muss sich vielmehr auf Kuba selbst und aus seiner Bevölkerung heraus entwickeln. Die Unterstützung zivilgesellschaftlichen Engagements und seiner Institutionen, der Entwicklung freier und unzensierter Medien sowie der demokratischen politischen Bewegungen ist zentral für die Herausbildung einer breiten gesellschaftlichen Basis für demokratischen Wandel und eine selbstbestimmte Zukunft des kubanischen Volkes.

Auf Kuba haben sich eine Reihe hoffnungsvoller Initiativen entwickelt, die unter hohem Risiko und mit großem Engagement für einen demokratischen Wandel eintreten. Sie gilt es zu unterstützen und mit ihnen muss ein kontinuierlicher Dialog gepflegt werden. Dazu gehören unter anderem die politischen Projekte „Varela“ und „Todos Cubanos“ um Oswaldo Payá Sardiñas, die soziale Frauenprojekte von „FLAMUR“ und die Bildungsprojekte der katholischen Kirche wie beispielsweise der „Verband der unabhängigen Bibliotheken“.

Angesichts der vorsichtigen wirtschaftlichen Reformen sollte der doppelte Dialogansatz um eine dritte, eigenständig betonte Dimension ergänzt werden, welche auf Öffnungssignale der kubanischen Seite antworten und zugleich als Scharnier zwischen den beiden anderen Zielbereichen – Staatsführung und Gesellschaft – dienen kann: Zur Verbesserung der wirtschaftlichen Lage und insbesondere der Versorgung der Bevölkerung sollte die wirtschaftliche Zusammenarbeit mit Kuba verstärkt werden. Eine Erhöhung der EZ-Mittel und gezielte Ermutigungen zu ausländischen Direktinvestitionen sollten allerdings schrittweise realisiert werden. In entsprechenden Schritten sollte Kuba gleichzeitig die Bildung freier Gewerkschaften akzeptieren, die Zahlung gerechter Löhne gewährleisten und die Wahrung zentraler Arbeiterrechte sicherstellen.

Das von den USA über Kuba verhängte Embargo und insbesondere seine 1996 erfolgte Verschärfung durch das Helms-Burton-Gesetz haben sich in den vergangenen Jahren als kontraproduktiv erwiesen. In Anbetracht der Zeichen vorsichtiger Öffnung auf Kuba sollten die USA gerade jetzt dazu ermutigt werden, ihre Blockadepolitik – und insbesondere die auch Unternehmen aus Drittstaaten beeinträchtigende Verschärfung – aufzugeben und sich der beschriebenen Dialog- und Kooperationsstrategie anzuschließen. Ein pragmatischer Kurs der USA gegenüber Kuba kann dazu beitragen, Handel zu schaffen, welcher dem wirtschaftlichen Aufbau und der Bevölkerung Kubas direkt zugute kommt. Der Zeitpunkt für eine solche Neuausrichtung der Kubapolitik ist mit dem Wechsel der Administration in den USA heute wesentlich günstiger als jemals zuvor.

Wege und Instrumente der Unterstützung des demokratischen Wandels auf Kuba

Auf allen drei Ebenen – im politischen Dialog auf allen staatlichen Ebenen, im Dialog mit und zur Unterstützung der Zivilgesellschaft sowie der demokratischen Opposition, im Bereich der wirtschaftlichen Kooperation – sollten schrittweise konkrete Projekte abgesprochen und umgesetzt werden. Bei Fortschritten sollte ihre Ausweitung kontinuierlich verfolgt werden.

Mit der Präsenz und dem Ausbau der Arbeit der politischen Stiftungen auf Kuba kann ein partnerschaftlicher und konstruktiver Dialog über die politischen und sozialen

Herausforderungen unserer Zeit begonnen werden. Insbesondere beim Aufbau eines pluralistischen Presse- und Medienwesens, im Hinblick auf die Vorbereitung und Durchführung demokratischer Wahlen sowie zur Schaffung eines Bewusstseins für Arbeiterrechte können unsere politischen Stiftungen theoretisches sowie praktisches Wissen vermitteln, Diskussionen anstoßen und die jeweils relevanten Akteure versammeln helfen. Die SPD sollte überdies die Initiative ergreifen und anregen, dass die Sozialistische Internationale eine Sondierungskommission nach Kuba schickt, um zu prüfen, ob und wann der Sozialdemokratischen Partei Kubas (unter dem Vorsitz von Vladimiro Roca Antúnez) sowie der sozialistischen Partei „Arco Progresista" (unter dem Vorsitz von Manuel Cuesta Morúa) ein Status zuerkannt werden kann.

Mit dem Abschluss eines Kulturabkommens und der baldigen Eröffnung eines Goetheinstituts kann der politische Dialog auf der kulturellen Ebene ergänzt und vertieft werden. Durch die früher sehr engen Beziehungen zur DDR haben viele KubanerInnen gute Deutschkenntnisse, an die mit der Errichtung einer deutschen Schule oder mit einem verstärkten Angebot von Deutschunterricht angeknüpft werden kann. Ebenso wichtig sind die Intensivierung des wissenschaftlichen Austausches, die Forderung nach einer Wiederaufnahme gerecht und transparent vergebener staatlicher Stipendien sowie der Wiedereinstieg in eine bilaterale wirtschaftlich-technische Zusammenarbeit.

Im Zusammenhang mit dem gesellschaftlichen und wirtschaftlichen Wandlungsprozess sollten Projekte entwickelt werden für eine Reform des gegenwärtigen Systems der dualen Währungen, für die Reform des Justiz- und Verwaltungswesens, für die Umstellung der sozialen Sicherung auf ein System der negativen Einkommensteuer, zur Entwicklung der Landwirtschaft sowie zugunsten der Verbesserung von wirtschaftlicher Produktivität und Nachhaltigkeit im Allgemeinen. Von großer Dringlichkeit sind zudem grundsätzliche Fragen der Verteilungs- und Leistungsgerechtigkeit.

Akute Hilfe bei der Bewältigung der immer wieder von tropischen Stürmen verursachten Schäden sollte kurzfristig und unbürokratisch angeboten werden.

Vielfältige Kontakte auf zivilgesellschaftlicher Ebene sollten angeregt und ausgebaut werden. Dazu gehören kommunale

Partnerschaften sowie solche zwischen Gewerkschaften, Verbänden und kulturellen Institutionen. Auch die Kontakte der Kirchen im Rahmen von Gemeindepartnerschaften, des ökumenischen Austauschs, in der diakonischen und Bildungsarbeit sind zu stärken.

Chancen jetzt nutzen!

Kuba ist in einer Übergangsphase. Raúl Castro scheint einen vorsichtigen Politikwechsel einzuläuten. Dabei ist zwar noch offen, wohin dieser Prozess führen wird, allerdings werden damit auch Chancen einer Entwicklung hin zu Demokratie und Rechtsstaatlichkeit eröffnet. Wir erwarten weitere maßgebliche Schritte zur Öffnung und Demokratisierung des Landes, wollen zu einer klaren und kohärenten EU-Politik gegenüber Kuba beitragen und werden die KubanerInnen bei der Gestaltung ihres künftigen Entwicklungsweges unterstützen.

Von Markus Meckel, MdB | Stand: Dezember 2008

Part 5: Cuba from a Czech and Latvian perspective

Martin Palouš:

Lecture "The Unfinished Dialogue between Vaclav Havel and Oswaldo Paya. Cuba in 2016."

Buenos Aires, CADAL

July 5, 2016

I. Introduction.

Thanks, something about CADAL, Instituto Havel, my participation at the Havel legacy institutions, Havel@80 - the Havel's legacy in the context of current political situation in the world. Cuba.

II. Paya – Havel letters (October 31, November 17, 2013) (Journal of Democracy (Vol. 15, Number 2, April 2004)

Context: Havel-Paya phone conversation (September 2002), The Cuban "black spring of 2003", Paya in Prague at Forum 2000 (October 2003)

Paya:

...The phase of Cuban history now coming to an end has been very complex in human terms, and another of the bitter fruits of this regime would be to continue pitting Cubans against one another over what has happened up to now. We would thus continue submitting ourselves to the hate and injustice that totalitarianism has sawn. Forgiveness and reconciliation are vital in this process of liberation, and that is why peaceful struggle is not only our method but our aim. We want to put violence, hatred and insults behind us once for all....

...I keep thinking about today's Czech Republic. You have achieved change and liberation. You have done it and, most importantly, done it on our own terms. We will achieve this in Cuba. We are already doing it, among Cubans, among everyone,

those of us, who live on the inside, and those who live in exile and are inseparable part of our nation….

…Therein lies the fundamental change that we seek – the participation of citizens in the political, economic, and cultural life of the country as free people…

…. The transition for Cuba will be a transition towards democracy, social justice, development, and peace. The human persons, family, and community will be most important, above and beyond any general model of how society ought to be organized….

Havel:

…Based on my experience, international solidarity is important at this time. Such solidarity should be expressed by free governments as well as by individuals. Democratic countries should

make their relations with the totalitarian political leadership conditional on the release of prisoners of conscience and on the relaxation of inhibitions on free nationwide discussion. Democratic countries should consider as their partners all democratically minded people, irrespective whether they hold any political offices....

...I would like to draw attention to an observation of mine: Whatever your merits, however brave and respectable as dissidents you may be, even though you may spent years in prison or written clever books – in spite of all that, pragmatic politicians in the democratic world may suspect that you are mere grumblers, inveterate complainers, slightly crazy and constantly carping. Such a suspicion might lead to the following opinion: We may support them symbolically, but from the point of view of realistic politics there is no

need to rely on them; they are not the right partners for us. And yet the opposite is true. It is important to convince politicians in democratic countries about this, which I have been trying for many years...

...The Velvet Revolution in Czechoslovakia caught us totally unprepared to take power from the hands of the regime which collapsed within a couple of weeks. If I would emphasize one thing in particular, it is this:

Each democrat who oppose a totalitarian regime should behave today as if power were to be handed over tomorrow.

We were caught by surprise at how fast the exhausted communist system collapsed, and we were not prepared for an immediate takeover of power. We were thus forced to make all essential decisions, under pressure of circumstances, in a matter of days – sometimes even hours. But it was precisely the first moments in the transfer of power that were the most important. At that time, decisions were made that would affect the fate of the country for years to come...

...Last but not least, it is also worth to considering who among the current politicians would make the best negotiating partners if the occasion for a handover of power should arise...

...The main thing, however, is for Cubans to be able to decide for themselves about their future – with whom and under what conditions they do or do not want to cooperate. This must be an un-manipulated decision made by Cubans alone. No country has the right to impose anything on you or to restrict your choices...

III. Cuba in 2016

1. The New US policies

The decision of the US and Cuban Governments to re-establish the diplomatic relations between the two countries has certainly added new dynamism to the debate on Cuba. The visit of President Obama to Havana – the first trip of the American head of state to Cuba since Calvin Coolidge in 1928 – was, indeed, a historical event. How to perceive all the changes taking place today after the decades of open hostility, indicating that even for the Caribbean island still ruled by the communist government that came there in power almost six decades ago, the Cold War seems to be finally over?

Two schools of thought are clashing here. The argument of the supporters of the new US policy towards Cuba is clear and simple: the policy of isolation practiced by the US Government in the past has not produced any positive results, so something else must be tried! Regardless of how strong the will to hold power and the intense survival instincts of the Cuban totalitarian regime are, there are a growing number of new elements characterizing the current

Cuban situation that are not and, by their very nature, cannot be under its control. In spite of all the efforts of the current power-holders to preserve the status quo the Cuban reality today is different from the past and is changing irreversibly with ever growing speed. Yoani Sanchez once said: “Cuba se cambia, and nobody can stop this trend!” The Government of the United States must depart in its policies towards Cuba for the basic fact that any society simply cannot remain the same forever. The constructive engagement of the Cuban Government, the re-establishment of diplomatic relationships between Cuba and the United States and their gradually renewed economic cooperation must be perceived just as a first, but absolutely necessary, step on a journey towards the accomplishment of the ultimate goal the US Government is pursuing here. Its new Cuba policy is certainly not to serve the US “national interests” only, but to enhance – in conformity with the fundamental American values and principles - freedom and prosperity of the Cuban people!

The opponents of the decision of President Obama to engage the current Cuban Government in the process of rapprochement believe to have now strong empirical evidence supporting their point of view. The new US policy is in place for almost eighteen months now and nothing has really changed in Cuba. It has generously offered a number of concessions and nothing has been obtained in return. Raul Castro's Government is still using its traditional methods of control and manipulation, fully endorsing the original ideological visions of Fidel and subscribing to the "revolutionary" program based on them.

The situation, in fact, has worsened for the Cuban people on the island since the "thaw" of the Cuba-US relations was announced. The level of repression used on a daily basis against the members of the awakening Cuban civil society has actually increased.[1]

Raul Castro may be advancing some rational reforms in order to address the basic problems of the Cuban people struggling day after day for their subsistence, and to adjust the Cuban economy to the challenges of the international system emerging in the beginning of the 21st century. It

[1] The source of information: the regular monthly reports published by Cuban Commission for Human Rights and National Reconciliation of Elizardo Sanchez or another independent organization "Hablemos Press".

doesn't mean, however, at all that he is ready to get rid of the "substance" of the Cuban "socialism" being "actualized" now; that he has changed his mind and ceased to be an "unrepentant" communist. He has never made even the smallest effort to extend his economic reform agenda into the political sphere. His principal goal is still what it has always been: to preserve the leading role of the Communist party using all available means at his disposal and oversee a smooth succession of power from the aging Moncadistas[2] - still its principal current holders - to the "politically conscious" members of younger generations.

2. Normalization of the EU-Cuba relations

A similar process of rapprochement with Cuba is on the way on the other side of Atlantic, as well. In February 2014, the Council of European Union Foreign Ministers agreed to start negotiations on a new bilateral agreement between the EU and Cuba. A diplomatic process got off the ground two months later. A declared common intention is to

[2] The revolutionaries accompanying young lawyer Fidel Castro in the attack against the Moncada barracks in 1953 who joined him in his mountain-based guerilla campaign started three years later.

overcome the unproductive and outdated legacies of the past; to adopt a new treaty which should govern the full scope of relations between the EU and Cuba (the political dialogue, cooperation, economic relations and trade) in a single agreement. It should be a standard legal instrument, similar to the treaties regulating the relations of the EU with other states of the ACP (African, Caribbean and Pacific) Group, all of which, unlike Cuba, are signatories of the "Cotonou Agreement"[3]. As far as the character of normalized" EU-Cuba relationships regulated by a new

[3] So called "Cotonou Agreement" (the ACP-EC Partnership Agreement, 2000/483/EC) is a treaty between the members of the African, Caribbean and Pacific Group of States (an organization of 79 African, Caribbean and Pacific States, including Cuba, created by the Georgetown Agreement in 1975 and having its Secretariat headquarters in Brussels) on the one side, and the European Community (now the EU) and its Member States on the other. It was signed in Cotonou, Benin, on June 23, 2000. Its main objectives are the reduction and eventual eradication of poverty and the gradual integration of African, Caribbean and Pacific States into the global economy, whilst adhering to the aims of sustainable development. It includes a strong political dimension consisting of regular political dialogue, peace-building policies, conflict prevention and resolution and promotion of human rights, democratic principles based on the rule of law and transparent and accountable governance. Its main financial instrument is the European Development Fund. Cuba first announced its intention to sign the Cotonou Agreement by a Verbal Note of February 2, 2000, but later withdrew its petition, arguing that the EU was setting unacceptable conditions for Cuba's accession with the attempt to infringe into Cuba's "internal affairs."

treaty is concerned, however, there is a profound difference between the expectations of the two "high contracting parties."

For the EU, the normalization of this relationship requires Cuba to finally start behaving like a "normal" ACP country; to open up its political and economic system and set itself on the way of national reconciliation: democracy, the rule of law, respect for human rights and economic prosperity. It implies that all general guidelines the EU has discussed internally and adopted for the various spheres of international cooperation with all other partners from the developing world (such as the "Strategic Framework and Action Plan on Human Rights and Democracy," adopted on 25 June 2012, for instance) are fully applicable. The revolutionary "exceptionalism" - still aggressively defended by the Cuban Government - is not to be tolerated anymore. It must be replaced unconditionally by the co-operation "in good faith", based on the joint recognition of all basic purposes and principles of international cooperation as stipulated by the Charter of the United Nations.

Having decided to engage Cuba, the EU is not at all resigning to its principles. Human rights are to "remain at the core of the relationship" between the EU and Cuba - the words of Catherine Ashton, the EU "Minister of Foreign Affairs"[4] in the spring of 2014. This recent decision to re-engage Cuba should not be understood as "a policy change from the past"! The EU 1996 "Common Position"[5] still remains in force! Therefore, the only concession made here is that the EU has agreed to start this process under the existing circumstances, despite the fact that the current state of human rights in Cuba is, for sure, far from satisfactory or even acceptable.

---

[4] The official title of the EU "foreign minister" is "High Representative of the European Union for Foreign Affairs and Security Policy and Vice-President of the European Commission".

[5] Reacting to the recent wave of gross human rights violations of human rights by the Cuba Government the EU adopted on 2 December 1996 the "Common position on Cuba" (agreed upon by the Council on the basis of Article J.2 of the Treaty on European Union) which explicitly states : *"...the objective of the EU in its relations with Cuba is to encourage a process of transition to pluralist democracy and respect for human rights and fundamental freedoms, as well as a sustainable recovery and improvement in the living standards of the Cuban people"*. It is the EU *"firm wish to be Cuba's partner in the progressive and irreversible opening of the Cuban economy"*[5], but the possibility of the *"full cooperation with Cuba will depend upon the improvements in human rights and political freedom..."* (96/697/CFSP).

The Cuban Government perceives the normalization of the relationship between the EU and Cuba through its traditional ideological lens and gives it an entirely different meaning. Departing from the sacrosanct principle of "non-intervention into domestic affairs of sovereign states" it sticks to the claim of having free hand to handle the process of Cuban transition in its own way; to keep in power all those who have been ruling in Cuba for decades and are responsible for the current highly unsatisfactory state of affairs on the island and replace them gradually by their heirs being recruited now among loyal and "politically conscious" members of younger generations.

But on the Cuban side, there has also been a positive signal sent to the EU. In the past the Cuban Government conditioned any future engagement with the EU on the strict demand that the said 1996 "Common Position" has to be first lifted. It has now agreed to start this process without any precondition and thus accepted the reality that the respect for human rights is a necessary condition for the EU if any progress is to be made in the bilateral relationship.

3. Sovereignty belongs to the Cuban People!

From the point of view of the activists of Cuban civil society the processes taking place today in the realm of international relations can play only a secondary - just enabling and certainly not decisive – role. The principal demand of those who belong to the Cuban "parallel polis"[6] - the mix of traditional human rights defenders, church activists, members of independent political parties of all colors from the left to the right; public intellectuals, journalists, artists or just open-minded and freedom-loving people without any specific skills or qualifications; blacks or whites, radicals or moderates – reminds us of the demands of East and Central European peoples made in the "miraculous year" of 1989. It is not just a minor improvement of the dysfunctional Cuban state. It is not just an "actualization" of Cuban "socialism." It is the respect for

[6] The term a "parallel polis" was invented in the milieu of the Czechoslovak Charter77. Its author is Václav Benda, whose seminal essay on this topic, written in 1978, initiated an important and rich discussion. Benda's essay "The Parallel Polis" and other contributions to this debate have been published in H. Gordon SKILLING and Paul WILSON (eds.), *Civic Freedom in Central Europe: Voices from Czechoslovakia* (Houndmills, Basingstoke, Hampshire: Macmillan, 1991).

inalienable human rights and freedoms of Cuban citizens! It is the re-opening of Cuban society being closed for almost six decades by the ruling regime! It is the restoration - by peaceful means and without violence - of sovereignty of the Cuban people! It is the recognition that the Cuban nation - as any other nation in the world – is endowed with "inalienable right to alter or change the shape of its Government"[7]; that it is up to Cubans only – and not in the hands of any foreign power or outside player- to decide the future of their homeland!

There is obviously one vital condition missing if the restoration of sovereignty of the Cuban people is to become reality and the process of democratization finally launched. It is the restitution of the Cuban "political nation" – the re-birth of a body politic in Cuba with a clear sense of purpose and vision, a community of freedom-loving people really showing the will to replace totalitarianism with democracy!

[7] The main demand of the campaign "Cuba Decide" is endorsed by the majority of groups of democratic opposition operating inside as well as outside of the island (http://cubadecide.com/).

But how is such a national revival to be achieved? Here lies the main challenge for the Cuban democratic opposition. And it is not only to resist, on a daily basis, all of their repressive action from the "ancient regime" still in power, as some of its courageous leaders seem to believe. It is to turn itself into a power capable of opening the way for Cubans to move from their bleak presence to a better future and propose a realistic scenario on how to get out of the current stalemate.

The problem is that the Cuban democratic opposition has always been highly fragmented and consisted of a number of competing factions. In spite of all sorts of calls for unification made in the past – and now again and again - it has not been able to do so. It has not yet offered a realistic program of democratic transformation acceptable for all Cubans as a viable political alternative to the current state of public matters on the island.

4. The relationship with the United States: a historical problem or a historical opportunity?

The persisting disunity within of the Cuban "parallel polis" has manifold reasons and this phenomenon certainly calls for a detailed and historically informed analysis. Such an enormous task obviously exceeds the scope of this short text. There is, however, a key external aspect contributing significantly to the current state of matters that must be reminded here: the complicated relationship between Cuba and the United States which has been developing throughout the 19th and 20th centuries.

The thing is that this relationship has always been, for obvious reasons, highly asymmetrical: on the one side the United States, the leading power of the liberal West with global responsibilities and also corresponding imperialistic ambitions and on the other side Cuba, a relatively small island country in the US neighborhood exposed historically to all sorts of direct or indirect forms of American influence and manipulations.

And here is how Jose Marti - the "apostle" of Cuban independence and one of the founding fathers of the modern Cuban nation - articulated the basic Cuban political problem in the last decades of the 19th century, the dilemma which stands in my view as the greatest challenge for the leaders of Cuban democratic opposition today. On the one hand there is the liberal tradition of the United States - "the land of the free and the home of the brave" in the words of the American National Anthem - undoubtedly the greatest inspiration of Cuban revolutionaries in the liberation struggles of the 19th century. On the other hand, however, an independent Cuban state must vehemently resist, said Marti, to be fully "Americanized", because its place is within the family of free Latin American nations. It should not be mentored endlessly by the United States or even subjected to the US hegemony. An independent Cuban state must be built as "a homeland for Cubans"; their "res publica" resting on their own spiritual and cultural traditions and resources; a vibrant democracy able to bring them into a better future together with other free nations, including Americans, while protecting and further cultivating their own unique Cuban identity.

Those who entered Havana triumphantly in the last day of 1958 in order to form there their "revolutionary" government – in power ever since - of course, immediately started to give this fundamental Cuban raison d'etat, articulated by Marti, their own twisted ideological interpretation. The unrelenting anti-Americanism has quickly become one of the principal political tools in the hands of Fidel Castro and his revolutionaries, to be used indiscriminately to suppress all their - both domestic and international – enemies. It was intentionally built by them into the very foundations of the Cuban totalitarian state. All their critics could then be stigmatized as traitors and persecuted as agents of American imperialism. The defense of the Cuban Revolution against the continuing acts of aggression committed by the United States could be declared as a principal patriotic duty of all Cubans. Whoever refused to support, or at least to get his/her behavior coordinated with this official line, could be eliminated from the Cuban public life at the discretion of the ruling power and severely punished.

And there is no need to add: the Cold War between the East and West which was in full swing in the moment of creation of Cuban "socialist" state, framed the designs of its founders with a highly favorable international environment and contributed decisively to its exceptional stability. In Europe, this conflict ended more than quarter century ago, but the political regime created by the Castro brothers and their cronies in the late 1950s is still here in the 2010s, still using its old, well-tested anti-American rhetoric to remain in power.

Does this new situation – in the middle of 2016, when the US and Cuban Embassies function again in the national capitals and after the historical trip of president Obama to Cuba in March - also open new opportunities for the Cuban democratic opposition? Definitely yes, but under one condition: that it is used creatively to overcome, once for all, the heavy burden of Fidel Castro's political legacy; that the difference in opinions as far as the new US policy toward Cuba is not perceived as a casus belli in its ranks, as a reason for escalation of "ideological" divisions within Cuban "parallel polis", but as a call for its unification. The dispute between the supporters and opponents of the steps taken by President Obama and his Administration - a manifestation of political pluralism that lies at the very core of American democracy; a continuing and never-ending struggle taking place on the US political scene which will only intensify in the year of presidential election 2016 – should not paralyze the possibility of dialogue among the Cuban democrats! Exactly on the contrary, it should be used by them as an opportunity to demonstrate that in spite of all their differences, they stand united by the common goal, able not only to talk to each other, but to act "in concert".

5. The reunification of Cuban nation

The most outspoken voices in the debate on Cuba in the United States have always belonged to the Cuban exiles who have arrived to US soil during more than six decades of the Castro dictatorship and have managed to create there a compact, politically influential and economically strong community - having more than two million members now and preserving a strong sense of national identity. What is their place within the ranks of Cuban democratic opposition?

There is no doubt that Cuban Americans are indispensable players in this collective effort: they represent an important part of the Cuban nation, and no one serious, as far as I know, has ever proposed that as exiles they should stay out of the struggle for democracy whose center is obviously at home. On the contrary as citizens of the United States they have a special responsibility - a significant role to play in the context of the future development of the endemically asymmetrical US-Cuba relations: to participate actively in the search of a new modus vivendi between Cuba and the United States; to initiate a national debate looking for a balanced, realistic answer to the old question raised by Jose Marti at the very beginning of a still unfinished journey for Cuban freedom and independence.

When "actualizing" Cuban socialism, the government of Raul Castro seems to be ready now to treat Cuban Americans with certain respect and not as traitors. He is even ready to welcome them as honored, valuable visitors on the island – as long as they are willing to stay out of Cuban politics and assume the role of providers of financial assistance to their relatives living there; as long as they are ready to accept the fact that a substantive portion of their money will end up in the coffers of Cuban totalitarian state and be used as a means for its survival.

At the same time, however, it is the restitution of the Cuban political nation composed of free-minded and committed people from both sides of the Straits of Florida, that the Castro regime should be afraid of more than anything else; that it is this task that should be perceived as the number one priority of Cuban Americans; that it is the main reason why all of them, democrats, republicans and independents, should join forces with those who struggle for Cuban freedom on the island and become active carriers of this unifying message.

But let's be honest and realistic here: to bridge the gap between those who have had to live for the decades exposed to the "totalitarian radiation"[8] and those who have not, is not an easy task. What is being opened here is a genuine "Pandora's Box", containing many unsettling questions - especially those touching upon the role of the Cuban-American exile community in the "crises" during the six decades of strained relationships between the United States and the Cuban totalitarian regime, and being systematically, and very "creatively", used by its propagandistic machinery.

What is required here is the courage to really start the process of genuine national reconciliation, to launch an inclusive national dialogue - involving Cubans of all generations living on the both sides of the Florida Straits, including those who some politicians would like to leave

[8] The term by Vaclav Havel.

behind: the former political prisoners of the communist regime. There should be no doubt that a true, undistorted record of their encounters with the Cuban recent history – the stories testifying to their patriotism and personal courage, full of suffering, but also of acts of their solidarity with all others who shared their fate - has an important place in the current process of Cuban liberation, bringing into the national debate about the Cuba's future the questions that should not be just forgotten, glossed over or treated - as some debaters seem to believe - as an old crap belonging to the history's garbage dump. Just the opposite is true. A new "social contract" among Cubans should, for sure, focus primarily on the Cuban future. But as it has been already convincingly demonstrated in many cases of countries in transition, it cannot be reached without recognition of and justice being served to what has happened in the past.

6. Encuentro National Cubano

At the same time when the US Secretary of State was visiting Havana to re-open the US Embassy in August of the last year, there was another Cuban event taking place in San

Juan, Puerto Rico worth of being paid attention to: the Cuban National Assembly (Encuentro Nacional Cubano), the constitunt meeting of a new platform of Cuban democratic opposition. The representatives of twenty three independent entities from Cuba and more than thirty exiled non-for-profits were in attendance. The objective of the "Encuentro" was to launch the debate on the common course of action in the current rapidly changing situation. For the first time the members of non-violent democratic opposition from the island and from exile met in such large numbers and talked to each other with a sense of common goals putting aside their differences, mutual grievances and recriminations. They all seemed to understand that it is their unity and a feasible political program for a new Cuba in the 21st century, what should become their most powerful weapon in their political, i.e. non-violent struggle against the obsolete totalitarian regime. The support pronounced publically by Diego Suarez - one of the veterans of the liberation struggle against "Castro-communism", now more than eighty years old - to Rosa Maria Paya – twenty seven years old daughter of Oswaldo Paya, whose Projecto Varella had been heavily criticized in the Miami conservative circles in the past – has become a kind of symbolical expression of new spirit of hope and determination which has prevailed at the San Juan meeting and is hopefully in action till today.

The Cuban National Assembly elected from its ranks nine members of its Coordinating Committee – five from the island and four from the exile – and entrusted them to represent the Assembly before the world and be in charge of organization of its activities.

The Assembly accepted the strategy of non-violence and peaceful struggle and associated itself with the "Agreement for Democracy" adopted by the major Cuban oppositional groups already in 1998. The Assembly has decided to launch public campaign for the plebiscite with legally binding results demanding free, fair and pluralistic election in Cuba; to look for all the possible way how to tear down the cyber wall which is still preventing the members of internal opposition to communicate effectively among themselves and with the world.

What has also been agreed on by the Assembly, were the fundamental, non-negotiable demands of Cuban democratic opposition: the release of all political prisoners;

the abolishment of the Cuban laws, suppressing the fundamental rights and freedoms of Cuban citizens; the recognition of the right to freedom of expression, freedom of press, freedom of assembly, freedom of association and peaceful demonstration; the recognition of the right to religious freedom and free choice of occupation; the recognition of the right to create political parties equally participating in political decisions; the holding of free and fair elections monitored by international observers.

It was also decided that the next Assembly will take place in the summer of 2016 with the basic task to discuss and adopt the National Cuban program for the 21st century. The next Assembly will also assess the current situation of Cuba as well as the results achieved. Based on this assessment, it should come with concrete proposals concerning both its future institutional set up and its further political steps and strategies.

7. The US and the EU "engagement" of Cuba Government and the basic philosophy of "Helsinki process" that brought the end of the Cold War in Europe

In spite of all the differences between the processes of “re-engagement” of Cuban Government recently started by both the United States and the European Union there is one significant similarity here. In both cases three separate “baskets” of problems are being put on the negotiation table in the context of new relationship to be created between the parties: peace and security, economic cooperation and human rights. Both the US and the EU argue - in line with their fundamental values and principles - that the third, i.e human rights basket is an indispensable part of the whole “package.” And both the US and the EU get the same reaction from the Cuban side: the bilateral relationship can be substantively improved, its new mutually beneficial forms agreed, even the proposed dialogue about human rights is possible, but under the condition of full respect for Cuban sovereignty and non-intervention to the Cuba’s internal affairs.

This argument is actually very similar to what the Western diplomats were hearing from their Eastern counterparts when the process of “détente” in Europe was launched in the 1970s. Isn’t it necessary then to draw inspiration from here in order to achieve in the today’s negations with the communist government of Cuba the desired results? Should not the governments of the United States and the EU insist that the Cuban state must not only honor its international obligations in the area of human rights if the negotiations are to move forward in the spirit of cooperation, but stop using the concept of state sovereignty in a way which is obsolete and out of step of current international law - recognizing as its emerging norms the concepts of “democratic entitlement” and “democratic legitimacy”? Should not they insist that any progress in negotiation can be made only after Cuba accepts the notion that the state sovereignty is not absolute or unconditional, because “Governments instituted among Men”, as American Declaration of Independence phrased it, derive their just power from the consent of the governed”? That the state sovereignty is always secondary and contingent to the sovereignty belonging to the people? Shouldn’t they insist that the independent voices of civil society must be also allowed - in an appropriate way - to participate in the process of “rapprochement” and turned into an indispensable “third” party to the agreement which will also be in charge of its implementation?

When in 1975, the Final Act of the Conference on Security and Co-operation in Europe was signed, there were also many skeptical voices, especially in the United States, that this deal between the East and West to secure the peaceful co-existence of states with "different social and political systems" was a victory of the Soviet leader Leonid Brezhnev and the ultimate confirmation of the status quo which was established in Europe as the result of the Second World War. But just the opposite turned out to be true. The third basket of the Helsinki Accords, however, opened the space for Czechoslovak Charter 77, The Polish KOR and later Solidarnosz, for the Helsinki Committees and other similar bodies emerging first in the Soviet Union itself and later throughout the whole region. It was the Western diplomats who sought and managed to secure for these civic initiatives, sometimes after a very hard fight, at least some level of international recognition. And it was this recognition what empowered them also domestically; what not only created a kind of protective shield against the excessive persecutions of their participants, but opened the way to the miraculous year of 1989 with its wave of peaceful and democratic revolutions which changed radically the political face of the whole region.

The diplomatic processes taking place around Cuba today call for exactly for the same strategy. The Cuban democratic opposition seems to be aware of it and there are multiple encouraging signs that that they are ready to step out internationally as a coherent enough and sufficiently organized body able to communicate effectively with its international partners; to present to them their own version of transition in Cuba; to comment on the deals which are on the table and bring to the consideration of diplomats and governmental experts their own inputs. What is necessary now is the clear commitment on the side of both American and European diplomats not to "re-engage" the Cuban Government only, but to be engaged actively, creatively and in the "Helsinki spirit" with the Cuban civil society, to seriously listen to their arguments and bring into the process of negotiation with the Cuban side also their communications.

8. In Conclusion

There are several signs of hope coming out this year that in spite of stubborn resistance by Cuban Government, the "Helsinki spirit" is waking up in the Cuban context. I will mention here only those that can be observed on the European side.

The negotiation between the EU and Cuba about a new bi-lateral treaty is followed closely by the European Parliament.

The conference "Quo Vadis Cuba?" was organized in Berlin and attracted a very good attention, offering an opportunity to a representative group of Cuban democratic opposition to send out its message.

The level of awareness what is at stake here is slowly rising. The trans-Atlantic dimension of the Cuban question – is there space here for some cooperation or co-ordination between the United States and the European Union in their processes of engaging of Cuban Government, for instance as far as the dialogue about human rights and assistance and political support of the Cuban democratic opposition is concerned? – is slowly getting ground and more attention.

But the most of work still remains to be done – the Cuban "parallel polis" composed of the people from the island and living in exile seems to be well aware of that and is determined more than ever to keep pushing. Let us hope that its international partners and supporter will hear this call and assist – inspired by the "Helsinki spirit" which changed Europe - the brave Cuban democrats in their continuing effort to finally tear down the last remaining "Berlin Wall".

Oskars Kastens:
Eastern European Lessons for "Freedom Island"

25 years have passed, since the collapse of the Berlin wall and Communist Regimes in Eastern Europe. Tremendous changes have transformed the political landscape in a region which once was regarded from an ideological point of view. Now it is fragmented into geographical areas – like Northern Europe (Baltic States), Central Europe (Visegrad countries), Eastern Europe (Ukraine), Balkan and Western Balkan countries (Albania, Bosnia and Herzegovina, Kosovo, Croatia, Macedonia, Montenegro and Serbia). The political landscape and elections in former Warsaw Pact countries are characterised by full spectrum of parties, from communist to extreme right.

However, due to the nature of new democracies, the countries stretching from Baltic to Adriatic Sea are experiencing similar patterns. According to Eurobarometer in 2013[9], in the "old" Northern and Western European democracies, trust in political parties never exceeds 40%. In Central and Eastern Europe, with Southern Europe, trust falls below the EU average (19%) except Hungary, Slovakia and Malta. In the Baltic States trust in parties varies from 9% to 17%. The lowest trust in political parties of new democracies is recorded in Slovenia, where only 5 percent of the population trust political parties. Many researchers emphasize the fact of a weak linkage between the voters and parties, as well as blurred ideological stances of the parties comparing to those in Western Europe.

However, despite the party system fragmentation, political volatility and disenchantment in promises made at pre-electoral period, Central and Eastern European countries are keeping up with democratic principles, which are rooted in peaceful "velvet" and "singing" revolutions. What are the

[9] Eurobarometer 79.3/2013 cited in: European Research Centre for Anti-Corruption and State-Building (ERCAS), Hertie School of Governance. Public Integrity and Trust in Europe, Policy Report commissioned by the Dutch Ministry of the Interior and Kingdom Relations (BZK), Berlin 2015, p.10.

lessons the Cuban and world leaders can learn from Central and Eastern European experience during the transition from totalitarian to multi-party political system?

First, in the framework of reform packages, Cubans are free to travel abroad without receiving permission from state authorities. More than half-a-million Cubans – 10% of the total workforce – are registered as self-employed, with the greatest weight in food preparation and sales, freight and passengers transport and the leasing of houses and rooms. In some regard, Cuba follows the footsteps of Yugoslavia's market socialism, featured by small private enterprises and large parts of agriculture given to private holdings and farmers. Unsurprisingly, reforms in both countries were entailed by economic hardships - by 1979 Yugoslavia's foreign debt was at about $20 billion[10], comparing to Cuba's $26 billion debt in 2015[11]. The gradual liberalisation of

[10]Susan L. Woodward. The West and the International Organisations, in: David A. Dyker, Ivan Vejvoda (eds.). Yugoslavia and After: A Study in Fragmentation, Despair and Rebirth, London/New York: Longman 1996, p.159.

[11]Central Intelligence Agency. Cuba, The World Fact Book, Washington D.C. 2017. Retrieved on January 4, 2017. From: https://www.cia.gov/ library /publications/the-world-factbook/geos/cu.html#.

administrative reins is suggesting that Cuba today shares some of the traits that we saw in the Central European dictatorships in the period before the fall of communism.

Carl Gershman, President of the National Endowment for Democracy, mentions there is "a limited increase in economic and cultural pluralism, even in the absence of political pluralism; a significant weakening of the regime's political legitimacy as a result of its economic failures and ideological exhaustion, even as it continues to mouth the old revolutionary rhetoric; a decrease in the internal cohesion and member loyalty of state-run mass organizations of youth, workers, and intellectuals"[12]. The international community has to seize every opportunity in supporting sporadic and disenchanted Cuban society groups emerging as the result of reforms.

At the same time, significant efforts should be made to engage Cuban political elites in international organizations,

[12]Carl Gershman. The New Fight: Cuba and the Movement for Democracy, World Affairs Journal, Winter 2016, p.2. Retrieved on January 4, 2017. From: http://www.worldaffairsjournal.org /article /new-fight-cuba-and-movement-democracy.

forums and to engender other forms of cooperation. One should not underestimate direct communication with peers from other countries with democratic traditions and values.

The Organization for Security and Co-operation in Europe (OSCE) is the world's largest regional security organization with 11 Asian and Mediterranean partner states for cooperation.[13] The Council of Europe (COE), the main human rights watchdog organization, has 47 member states and six observer states from Asia, Middle East and North America.[14] Observer or partner state status in both organizations would be a positive sign of a growing rapprochement between Cuba and European organizations. The transition to democracy is an arduous process. The work with political elites can mitigate risks in Cuba on her way to becoming a real Freedom Island.

Second, it is important to identify preconditions for "transferring" democratic processes, which shaped Eastern European countries, to the creation of functioning

[13] OSCE. Retrieved on January 4, 2017. From: http://www.osce.org/.
[14] COE. Retrieved on January 4, 2017. From: https://www.coe.int/en/.

democracy, civil society and political freedom in future Cuba. One of major priorities is consistent support for the strengthening of institutions, which will emerge as the result of democratic transition (i.e. NGOs, political parties and human rights organisations). After the fall of Communism, Central and Eastern European countries received munificent financial aid to strengthen the public sector to fight corruption and establish the rule of law and human rights institutions. The recent examples of international organizations activities to ensure Myanmar's successful re-integration into the family of democratic ASEAN countries can serve as a model for Cuba. The European Union can play an essential role in these efforts with its well-established development assistance programs to new democracies. The United States is vital with its over two million huge Cuban diaspora, which will contribute to the transition to democratic society.

Thirdly, one should not forget that the only institution in Cuba remaining independent of the Communist government is the Catholic Church. It represents about 60 percent of the country's population. Following constitutional amendments a quarter century ago, the government declared Cuba a secular state rather than an atheist state. In this regard, the parallels can be drawn with Poland in the 1980s, where the Polish Church and the Pope lent powerful legitimacy to the trade union *Solidarnosc* – the first independent mass movement in the communist world. John Paul II in his encyclical letter *"Redemptor Hominis"*[15] reflected on human rights by concluding that "the essential sense of the State, as a political community, consists in that the society and people composing it are master and sovereign of their own destiny. This sense remains unrealized if, instead of the exercise of power with the moral participation of the society or people, what we see is the imposition of power by a certain group upon all the other members of the society".

Nowadays Pope Francis and former Cuban Cardinal Jaime Ortega are credited with engagement in the historic rapprochement between the USA and Cuba, which began in

---

[15]John Paul II, Encyclical letter *"Redemptor hominis"*, Vatican City: *Libreria Editrice Vaticana*, March 4, 1979, p.23. Retrieved on January 4, 2017. From: http://w2.vatican.va/content/john-paul-ii/en/ encyclicals/documents/hf_jp-ii_enc_04031979_redemptor-hominis.html.

2014. A more proactive role of the Catholic Church definitely can be a catalyst for human rights in Cuba.

Part 6: Initiatives for Change in Cuba

Martin Palouš:
The Role of Vaclav Havel Legacy Institutions in the Current Cuban Debate and the Proposed Cuba-Related Activities in 2016

I. Who is who?

a.) **Vaclav Havel Library**

(VHL, http://www.vaclavhavel-knihovna.org/en)

A principal co-ordination center of all Havel-related activities not only in the Czech Republic but around the world (a primary database for research projects, a central hub of all activities in the field of public advocacy, human rights diplomacy).

b.) **Vaclav Havel Library Foundation**

(VHLF, http://www.vhlf.org/)

A US non-for profit (501c3) organization co-operating closely with Vaclav Havel Library in Prague and acting as co-ordination center all Havel-related activities in North America.

c.) **Vaclav Havel Program for Human Rights and Diplomacy** at Stephen Green School of International and Public Affairs at Florida International University FIU (VHP, http://havel.fiu.edu/)[16]

[16]**Vaclav Havel Program for Human Rights and Diplomacy** was created in 2013 to strengthen the academic dimension of all the existing endeavors to preserve the Havel's legacy internationally and respond to the need to integrate Havel's ideas and themes into a broader context of current public discourse, political philosophy and/or political science, as a part of Stephen Green School for Public and International Affairs (SIPA) at Florida International University. Vaclav Havel Program at FIU is an institution still in *statu nascendi*, but it has been identified as one of the priorities in the SIPA's future development. The expectation is that it will bring into SIPA's impressive interdisciplinary structure a specific Central European focus. The synergies will be generated by close cooperation between this initiative and already existing SIPA programs, enhanced academic opportunities for students and high quality scholarship and research. The intention is to build – consistently with the mission statement of SIPA itself – one more bridge between life of the university devoted to higher education and science, and the practical world consisting of engaged citizens, public intellectuals, human rights defenders, artists, entrepreneurs and of course, politicians. Here is what is promised in the Vaclav Havel Program's Mission Statement: *"...to study and explore the politics of human rights, the processes of democratization in societies that were once under autocratic governments, and the experiences of societies currently in transition around the world. Our experiential basis and point of departure is Eastern and Central Europe, the home of Vaclav Havel. Our ambition is to foster partnerships, international dialogue and greater global exchange in the areas of human rights, democratization and diplomacy."* Here are six areas of interests defined for its future activities:<

1. Central European Political Thought and Philosophy

d.) **International Platform for Human Rights in Cuba (IPHRC)**

A US non-for profit (501c3) organization based in Miami closely cooperating with Vaclav Havel Center at FIU, active in the field of advocacy for human rights, serving as principal liaison with the activists of Cuban civil society organizations both in exile and on the island.

II. The Cuba-related activities in 2015

Vaclav Havel Library

The theme of Cuba is generally perceived, both at home, but also internationally, as an intrinsic part of Havel's political legacy. There are several points on its Cuba sheet in 2015 to be highlighted:

---

2. Contemporary History of Central Europe
3. Central European Culture, Literature and Art
4. International Human Rights and Civil Society
5. Democratic Transitions in the 20th and the 21st Century
6. World Politics, International Law and National Interest of Small States in the 21st Century.

   Currently the Vaclav Havel Program is taking the lead in the launch of an undergraduate Certificate in Human Rights and Political Transitions to offer students an introduction to human rights as a concept of justice in a globalized, increasingly complex world.

1. The gathering of all necessarily documents and data to be used in a book on Vaclav Havel Foreign Policies planned to be published in 2016 under the occasion of Vaclav Havel 80th birthday;

2. The visit of Director of VHL Michael Zantovsky to FIU, where he lectured about the Central European experience of transition as a part of program of Vaclav Havel Program *"Preparing Miami for Transition in Cuba"*, financed by Knight Foundation;

3. The participation of Director of VHL Michael Zantovsky at the conference in Berlin *"Quo Vadis Cuba?"* organized by Konrad Adenauer Stiftung together with VHP and IPHRC and at the cultural event *"Voices of Today's Cuba"* hosted by Czech Center in Berlin;

4. The lecture of Rosa Maria Payá at VHL in Prague followed by a discussion about the current Cuban situation. Rosa Maria Payá was also received under this occasion by Speaker of the Czech Parliament Jan Hamacek and made a couple of interviews for the Czech media.

Vaclav Havel Program for Human Rights and Diplomacy at FIU

The two year project *"Preparing Miami for Transition in Cuba"* supported by Knight Foundation has enabled VHP to establish itself as a respected focal point for the public debates about the current Cuban political situation and possible scenarios for the Cuba's future in the Miami area. The confrontation of experience of transition from totalitarianism to democracy in East Central Europe with the perspectives of Cuban democratic opposition has proven itself as a great impulse for a real dialogue between those who belong to the different "schools of thought" in the context of Cuban transition and thus advocating different policies.

The decision of President Obama to "re-engage" the Cuban totalitarian regime – which has in the ranks of Cuban democratic opposition not only supporters, but a number of opponents - only underlined the importance of such dialogues and exchanges of opinion. Vaclav Havel Program at FIU is now known as a place having the capability to serve as their facilitator.

The lecture of Pavel Telicka - a member of European Parliament and vice-chair of its liberal group ALDE - offered an opportunity for FIU students as well as for a larger Cuban American audience to participate at a debate about the European perspectives as far as the current Cuban situation is concerned. It highlighted the need to open efficient communication between the EU and the members of Cuban democratic opposition.

International Platform for Human Rights in Cuba

Thanks to the grant from National Endowment for Democracy (NED) IPHRC was able to fully accomplish its goals set in two main areas of its activities:

1. To lend itself as a facilitator of better communication between the different groups within the ranks of Cuban democratic opposition, namely in the area of international relations; to assist in formulating its "foreign policies" - in setting the realistic goals in this area, bearing in mind the instruments at its disposal for their implementation.

Martin Palouš was invited as only foreign speaker to participate at the first Cuban National Assembly that took place in August in San Juan, Puerto Rico and addressed the Assembly at its final dinner.

2. To initiate and organize together with Konrad Adenauer Stiftung an international conference in Berlin *"Quo Vadis Cuba?"* which turned out to be a great success.

Besides the active Cuban participants in the four panels of the conference - selected after thorough consultations with IPHRC and VHP by Konrad Adenauer Stiftung - there were other Cubans joining the debates at the conference: a group of Cuban human rights activists who arrived to Berlin from Prague after they had absolved there a training program organized by People in Need Foundation; a group of Cuban musicians (rockers and rappers) sponsored by Cuban Soul Foundation, representing "new voices of Cuba" – a society which is slowly getting out from the cage built for its citizens by Fidel Castro and his revolutionaries and seeking the new forms of its self-expression.

What was originally planned as a one and half day conference grew up in the end to three full days of Cuba-related events in Berlin. Both the activities which were added to the program by a non-for profit organization Global

Panel Foundation (opening reception, Public Policy Lunch attended by Cubans and staffers from Bundestag; Public Policy Dinner devoted to the Cuban situation attended by a group of public intellectuals and opinion makers; Public Policy Lunch and two discussion sessions about strategies of transition between the Cubans and the members of Global Panel Foundation) and the cultural event *"Voices of Today's Cuba"* hosted by Czech Center in Berlin managed to send out a clear message: the Cuban democratic transition is a highly relevant theme deserving serious attention of European public; calling for international solidarity with Cubans struggling for freedom and for thoughtful and creative diplomatic action.

Both, Konrad Adenauer Stiftung and Global Panel Foundation have indicated that, based on the positive Berlin experience, they are ready to consider our proposals for Cuba-related projects and start discussing about forms of our future co-operation. There is also a new strategic partnership being built after Berlin between VHP and the People in Need Foundation.

III. The Working Plan for 2016

Vaclav Havel Library and Vaclav Havel Library Foundation

VHL and VHLF – that have recently reached the agreement to deepen their institutional bonds and increase the cohesion of their activities - will co-operate on the project of book Vaclav Havel Foreign Policies. Cuba will be highlighted here as a case illustrating the Czech current dilemmas arising in search for the right mix of foreign policy driven by human rights concerns and so called economic diplomacy.

In this context Cuba will also appear as a theme in the planned club activities of VHL in and will remain in the focus of the VHL's both domestic and international public advocacy.

VHP will prepare the important input for this book project: it will collect and organize all the documents and other information available related to the visit to Miami which was a part of the last official trip of Vaclav Havel to the United States as President of the Czech Republic in September of 2002 and had also a strong Cuban component.

The projects of global digital library and e-learning about Havel are being discussed now by VHL and VHLF with several potential donors. VHP will also participate in the debate about these projects and ensuing preparatory works with the specific focus on their Cuban dimensions.

Vaclav Havel Program for Human Rights and Diplomacy at FIU and International

Platform for Human Rights in Cuba

1. With regards to the fact that VHP is firmly established now as one of the focal points of the on-going debate about Cuba in the Miami area, VHP and IPHRC have the potential and are ready to cooperate with every player in the field from the left to the right, from the island and from the exile community, but first of all with Coordination Commission of Encuentro Cubano Nacional. Our principal goals here are:

a.) To support Second Encuentro Cubano Nacional being planned for the first half of the next year;

b.) To prepare special training programs for Cuban Democratic Opposition "tailored" according to the specific requirements of their submitters;

c.) To start the phase II of its project *"Preparing Miami for Transition of Cuba"*.

As far as a.): VHP is ready to offer its capacity and convening power to assist the Coordination Commission of Encuentro Cubano Nacional to fulfill its principal task which is to prepare successfully its second meeting. If it is found agreeable by it members, VHP is ready to serve as its neutral hosting place. It can also be used during the preparatory talks and in process of drafting of conference materials as an intermediary, an informed, but unbiased "third party", an honest broker, acceptable for all the parties involved - often subscribing to the different schools of thought and seeing the situation from their specific perspectives.

As far as b.): Special training programs of VHP will depart from the Central European transitional experience (VHP is relying here on the cooperation with PINF which has occupied itself with this theme in the past and published some very useful materials about it, available both in English and Spanish). At the same time these programs will largely benefit from the fact that VHP as a part of SIPA is now taking the lead in the launch of an undergraduate Certificate in Human Rights and Political Transitions. CANF has already asked VHP to come up with a concrete proposal and its realization is now a matter of further discussions.

As far as c.): After the successful completion of project *"Preparing Miami for Transition in Cuba"* its phase II is being prepared. Our plan is to include also the grand theme of Cuban national dialogue and reconciliation. What we want here is to organize a series of seminars and public debates focused not only on basic questions of transition to democracy, but also on elementary methodological problems of contemporary history connected necessarily with it. What appears absolutely necessary is to enlarge the historical horizon in which the debate about the recent past of Cuba is taking place; to bring in also the experts from the outside world (the Czech Post Bellum organization comes immediately to my mind) dealing with the similar issues as Cubans to Miami; to let them explain their approaches and lay out their experience and the result achieved. VHP intends to submit the proposal for *"Preparing Miami for*

Transition of Cuba II" to Knight Foundation within the next few weeks.

2. IPHRC will be also asking in the beginning of 2016 for the extension of the grant of NED focused on international dimension of the activities of Cuban democratic opposition. The project to be submitted will emphasize the need to strengthen the cooperation with VHP and is going to be focused on the following areas:

a.) another new round of communications (enabled by our cooperation with the group of European liberals ALDE) with the European Parliament about the state of negotiations of a new treaty between Cuba and the EU;

b.) the follow-ups of the Berlin conference: the continuation of the debate about the "Helsinki character" of current EU-Cuba and the US-Cuba "re-engagements" – in Brussels, in several other European capitals and in the United States - emphasizing the need for stronger support of civil society participating legitimately at "rapprochement" with the Cuban totalitarian state and also the need for more intensive transatlantic cooperation in this area;

c.) opening of a debate with all essential strategic partners about the forms of support of independent Cuban civil society in the current situation; mediation of efficient communication in this politically sensitive area; generation of qualified analytical input concerning this topic for the major donors operating in public sector as well as private foundations;

d.) the enlargement of space of the IPHRC operation: our intention is to start a round of consultation - in close coordination with our main Cuban partners - in the selected Latin American capitals and promote also there the "spirit of Helsinki" as a leading inspiration for the innovative approaches to the Cuban question corresponding to current dynamically evolving international situation.

Boris Luis Santa Coloma: Radio Cuba Dialoga

This is a project aimed at building bridges between the general populace and the Cuban peaceful opposition. Its main objective is to instill in average citizens the idea that opposition members can also be their spokespeople. This in turn will contribute to strengthen the opposition's own notions about their role as carriers of a popular mandate for the introduction of changes within Cuban society. After the fall of the Wall the East German media looked after a model and find it in the West German media. **RADIO CUBA DIALOGA** aimed also to become a model for the communist media at the beginning of the reform process in Cuba.

Despite other radio stations that reach the island, this project is not directed to preach to the choir. **Radio Cuba Dialoga** has an endogenous component because it stimulates dialogue between Cubans inside as well as outside. **Radio Cuba Dialoga** facilitates the peaceful approach between different sectors of the Cuban nation for a future opening process and political dialogue.

Radio Cuba Dialoga would be broadcasted from Europe twice a week to Cuba through the FM radio station RADIO RITMO 102.5, WIPK. It is a bilingual radio station located in Summerland Key. RADIO RITMO covers Homestead, the Florida Keys, many Caribbean Islands and the Cuban northern coast. There are a lot of Cuban listeners, as evidenced by few feedbacks in form of letters from the Island.

Hana Jakrlova:

Cuba: Before the Dawn

Cuba: Before the Dawn

International Art Exhibition | Book | Multimedia Project

Cuba: Before the Dawn is an **art project reflecting on Cuban reality** through works of **independent Cuban and international artists**. The project will result in exhibitions presenting photography, multimedia and conceptual works, as well as performance and book publications.

Cuba: Before the Dawn is nonpolitical project based in belief that art can be agent of change. Vaclav Havel was an artist before he became politician; in *Disturbing the Peace* he meditates on the social and political role of art. Havel was an advocate for democracy in Cuba and global responsibility, and his work is testament to the importance of artists in times of authoritarianism. Like Vaclav Havel, **we believe that art can promote real change**.

Cuba: Before the Dawn will be the first in **series of annual art exhibitions *'Before the Dawn'* from and about non-democratic countries**. Young people living in democracies often don't remember the totalitarian regime, while older generation sometimes forgets or relativises the past. With non-democratic tendencies on the rise around the world, *'Before the Dawn'* project will not only bring attention to and solidarity with people in dictatorships, but it will also have an educational aspect, as a powerful reminder of where ignoring democratic principles can lead.

The title of the project *'Before the Dawn'* is a nod to Cuban dissident writer Reinaldo Arenas and his novel *Before Night Falls,* which describes persecution of the artist by the Cuban regime.

The project is organised in partnership with *Amnesty International* and *Art for Amnesty Prague*.

<u>Cuba: Before the Dawn - Project Outline:</u>

I. *Cuba Now*

Photography Book *(ready for publication)*

Cuba today: daily life of people and their struggle captured in art documentary photography, showing Cuban reality in urban areas as well as in the country and across the section of Cuban society.

II. *Musica o Muerte*

Multimedia Project *(ready for post-production)*
The video project shows power of art against dictatorship - Cuban musicians opposing the regime. From *'los frikis'* who self-infected with HIV in the 90-ies as a protest and desire to live in freedom, to current days musicians *Porno Para Riccardo* known for their persecution and texts criticising the establishment.

III. *Cuba Libre*

Short Film *(ready for post-production* - video trailer available*)*

Cuba Libre captures testimonies of Cuban ex-political prisoners. The real depth of current change in Cuba is unclear, and for successful transition from dictatorship to democracy it is essential for Cubans to know their past. The story of Cuban ex-political prisoners jailed for 20 to 30 years in is largely untold.

IV. *Cuba Inside Out*

International Exhibition *(in progress)*

The multi-layered exhibition will reflect on Cuban reality from within and outside of the island through works of Cuban and international artists, thus presenting an independent perspective and creating a dialogue. The exhibition will take place in public places and / or in exhibition spaces. The 'show bubbles' will present installations, visual and multi-media presentations and photography works.

Visuals: Example of 'exhibiton bubbles' of Cuba Before the Dawn project in public spaces.

V. *Responsible Guide to Cuba: Not a Useful Idiot*

Travel App / Guidebook - *Additional outcome (in progress)*

A 'Lonely Planet' type of guide for people who want to support democracy when visiting Cuba, in form of a 'soft and safe' activism. The 'tourist's guide book of the 21st century' is based on the premise that **in our era of massive Internet activity, there is a significant power in personal involvement**. While it is essential that people around the world support human rights online, the significance of direct action is equally important but often more difficult. While travelling to non democratic countries, visitors frequently **unwillingly support the establishment rather then the people oppressed by the regime**.

The idea of the guide book is to suggest specific ways how to support ordinary people and human rights while visiting Cuba. Example: Every Sunday, a peaceful demonstration of *'Ladies in White'* takes place in Havana. If foreigners begun showing up, it could give a signal to the Cuban government, heavily relying on the money from tourism, that visitors care about the situation in the country. That could not only promote change in Cuba, but also signal to international politicians not to ignore the human rights issues in Cuba.

Responsible Guide to Cuba: Not a Useful Idiot will be the first in series of guides from various totalitarian countries. Except being a useful tool for responsible travellers, it will also have a strong educational aspect.

VI. Time Frame

Cuba: Before the Dawn will take place in mid 2017. The first stage of the project - *Cuba Now* photography book, *Musica o Muerte* multimedia project and *Cuba Libre* short film - will be completed by June 2017 and become part of the final exhibition *Cuba: Before the Dawn.*

There is only one Art, whose sole criterion is the power, the authenticity, the revelatory insight, the courage and suggestiveness with which it seeks the truth.
Vaclav Havel

Part II: About the Authors

Markus Meckel:

Biography*

Markus Meckel (born August 18, 1952) is a German theologian and politician. He was the penultimate foreign minister of the GDR and a member of the German Bundestag.

Markus Meckel was born on August 18, 1952 in Müncheberg, Brandenburg. He had to leave high school in 1969 for political reasons. From 1969 to 1971, he studied at the theological seminary *"Kirchliches Oberseminar Hermannswerder"*, receiving the parochially recognized entrance qualification *"Abitur"*. From 1971 to 1978, Meckel studied theology in Naumburg and Berlin.

Meckel had already been involved with domestic opposition to the East German Communist regime since the 1970s. In October 1989, he initiated the establishment of the Social Democratic Party in the GDR (SDP) together with Martin Gutzeit. From 23 February 1990 up to the merger with the West German SPD on 27 September 1990, he was deputy SDP party chairman. After the resignation of Ibrahim Böhme, who was accused of collaborating with the Stasi, he was acting chairman from 26 March to 10 June 1990.

In the GDR's first free elections in March 1990, Meckel was elected to Parliament. On 12 April 1990, he became the Minister of Foreign Affairs in the government of Prime Minister Lothar de Maizière (CDU). In his term of office, he frequently worked with Hans Dietrich Genscher, as he was one of the representatives of the two German states during the *Two Plus Four Negotiations* with the victors of the Second World War over a Final Peace Treaty. It was this treaty which paved the way to the reunification of Germany. On 20 August 1990, Meckel, together with the Social Democratic ministers, withdrew from the cabinet. The Ministry of Foreign Affairs was taken over by de Maizière himself.

After Germany was reunified on 3 October 1990, Meckel became a member of German Bundestag. From 1992 to 1994 he initiated the historical commission on the aftermath of the SED dictatorship in Germany and acted as spokesperson of the SPD parliamentary group. From 1994 onwards, he launched the follow-up project *"Stiftung*

Aufarbeitung" dealing with the effects of the East German dictatorship on the German process of reunification. There, he again served as the spokesman for the SPD's delegation.

In the Bundestag, Meckel focuses on European politics and German-Polish relations. Furthermore, since 1994 he is the chairman of the German-Polish Parliamentary Group. Since 1998 he is director/conductor of the German parliamentary delegation to NATO. From November 2000 until November 2002, he was vice-president of the parliamentary assembly of NATO.

Meckel is an advisory chairman of the Foundation for the Processing of the SED Dictatorship and besides member of the adviser of the Federal Authority for the Processing of GDR State Intelligence Files/BStU.

Minister Meckel is a Member of the Board of the Global Panel Foundation.

Markus Meckel is married the third time and has six children.

*Retrieved on Oct 27, 2016. From: https://en.wikipedia.org /wiki/Markus_Meckel (modified)

Martin Palouš:
Biography

Martin Palouš studied Natural Science, Philosophy and International Law. In 1974 he received Doctorate of Natural Sciences (RNDr). In 2001 he earned Higher Doctorate in Political Science/Philosophy (Associate Professorship at Charles University). In 2007 he got PhD in Public International Law at Masaryk University in Brno after the succesful defence of his doctoral thesis Freedom of Expression in the European Court of Human Rights. All academic degrees of Martin Palous received in the Czech Republic have been scrutinized and approved by a specialized independent agency in Florida, hired for this purpose by the FIU in the fall of 2010.

Since January of 2011, Martin Palous is Senior Fellow and Director of Vaclav Havel Program for Human Rights and Diplomacy at School of International and Public Affairs at Florida International University. He is also President of Vaclav Havel Library Foundation and President of International Platform for Human Rights in Cuba. He belonged to the original signatories of Charter 77, served as its spokesperson in 1986 and participated at the creation of Civic Forum during the Velvet Revolution (November 1989). After the fall of Communism he was a member of Parlament (1990), Deputy Minister for Foreign Affairs (1990-1992, 1998-2001), Ambassador of the Czech Republic to the United States (2001-2005) and Permanent Representative of the Czech Republic to the United Nations (2006-2011).

Martin Palous has rich academic praxis for more than 25 years. He has lectured at many universities both in the Czech Republic and in the world (particularly in the United States) and is author of numerous publications in the area of political philosophy, contemporary history, international relations and international law. (for instance: the chapter on the Czech Republic in the European Commission publication Democratization in Central and Eastern Europe (1998); Totalitarianism and Authoritarianism, in the Encyclopedia of Violence, Peace and Conflict (1999, 2nd ed. 2008); Between Idealism and Realism: Reflections on the Political Landscape of Postcommunism, in Between Past and Future; The Revolutions of 1989 and their Aftermath (2000), What Kind of God Does Human Rights Require?, in Does Human Rights

Need God? (2005); Common Sense and the Rule of Law, in Philosophy, Literature and Politics (2005); Jan Patočka's Socratic Message for the 21st Century, in: eds. Ivan Chvatik and Erica Abrams, Jan Patočka and the Heritage of Phenomenology (2011); Revolutions and Revolutionaries, Lessons of the Years of Crises, in: ed. Vladimir Tismaneanu, Promises of 1968. Crisis, Illusion, Utopia,(2011). He is a Member of the Prague Society for International Cooperation.

Boris Luis Santa Coloma: Biography

Boris Luis Santa Coloma

Master´s degree on Foreign Affairs

University of Havana

Mr. Boris Luis Santa Coloma is a radio journalist based in Berlin, as well as a strong activist and advocate for human rights. As one of the voices of the Cuban opposition in Germany, he promoted various initiatives towards respecting fundamental rights and civil liberties. SANTA COLOMA studied foreign languages (German & English) and foreign policy in Cuba.

From 1985-1990: Press Attaché at the Cuban Embassy in East Germany. In 1989, he witnessed the fall of the Berlin Wall. In 1990, he returned to Cuba. He was prosecuted when he advocated for a peaceful transition to democracy. In 1991, SANTA COLOMA fled to Germany into exile, where as a radio journalist he informed the Cuban audience about experiences in the process of democratic transition in Eastern Europe.

In 1998, he became a German citizen. He joined conferences and exchanges of experience in Poland, Hungary, Slovakia and the Czech Republic.

Reinhard Weißhuhn: Biography*

Reinhard Weißhuhn (*April 4, 1951 in Dresden) is a former representative of citizens' movement in the German Democratic Republic (GDR). He is a research associate of the Alliance '90/The Greens Fraction (*Bündnis 90/Die Grünen*) in the German Bundestag.

Reinhard Weißhuhn grew up in Saxony and in Weimar. His father was a journalist and his mother was a librarian. Having completed a secondary school in Weimar, from 1969 to 1973 Weisshuhn studied architecture and urbanism at the local university. After the graduation, he worked as an urbanist in the Council of the Borough of Berlin-Prenzlauer Berg. The communist regime responded to his autonomous cultural work in the residential area, his exchanges with artists of the Central and Eastern Europe and his engagement in the opposition movement by putting obstacles in the way of his career progression and by restrictions on his freedom of movement.

From 1975 he collaborated with György Dalos on the recommendation of Jürgen Fuchs. In 1978 the German Ministry of State Security initiated the so-called Operational procedure (*Operativer Vorgang*) against him. In that year he came to the Academy of Architecture and Civil Engineering of the GDR (*Bauakademie der DDR*) where he could work as a research and documentation engineer for several years. In that period he was translating texts of the Hungarian opposition movement for West German publications and organizing lectures in East Berlin. In 1985 he became an architect of the Protestant charity organization *Diakonisches Werk*.

He is one of the founders of the Initiative Peace and Human Rights (*Initiative Frieden und Menschenrechte* - IFM) and in the last years of the GDR existence he was a co-publisher together with Gerd Poppe of important opposition publications (incl. *grenzfall*, *fußnote*[3] and *Ostkreuz*) and he coordinated joint declarations of Central-and-Eastern-European anti-communist resistance movement. After the IFM opening in March 1989 he was a spokesman and one of the leaders of the Civil Rights Association

(*Bürgerrechtsvereinigung*). In 1990 he represented the IFM in the Central Round Table (*Zentraler Runder Tisch*). In the democratically-elected People's Chamber (*Volkskammer*) he collaborated with the Alliance '90 fraction. Then he came to the German Bundestag as a foreign-policy research associate. At first he worked for Gerd Poppe, later for Joschka Fischer and his fraction. In 1992 he was a member of Alliance '90 negotiation group for the preparation of the association agreement with the Greens. In 1993 he contributed on the European Programme of this Alliance. His political commitment has human rights and protection of minorities as its major issues. Since 2009 he has been a member of the board of the registered association *Robert-Havemann-Gesellschaft*.

*Retrieved on Oct 27, 2016. From:
https://de.wikipedia.org/wiki/Reinhard_Wei%C3%9Fhuhn
(modified & translated into English)

Hana Jakrlova: Biography

Hana Jakrlova is a Czech artist and curator living in Prague and New York. Her photography, film and curatorial work address issues of identity and freedom.

Hana's first major project *In the Meantime: Europe* documented the continent after the fall of Berlin Wall, capturing the identity of formerly divided Europe. The following project *Big Sister* focused on ways in which the Internet has transformed our world. Both series came out as photography books published by British, Dutch, Czech and French publishers (Eric Franck Fine Art, Schilt Publishing, Kant Publishing, Images en Manoeuvres Editions). Documentary film *Big Sister: Because of You* was produced together with XTV Production, Italy.

Mrs. Jakrlova's following documentary projects explored reality in countries transitioning from totalitarianism to democracy. Driven by her experience of growing up in communist Czechoslovakia, Hana worked in Russia, Serbia, Albania, Georgia, Burma and China, capturing life in (post)totalitarian countries.

In her recent project from Cuba, Hana focused on the country in transition and documented Cubans' reality and struggle for freedom. The first part of the series, *La Otra Cuba*, explores the world of ordinary people and activists, while the second part, *Cuban Disneyland*, documents an old government theme park. The multimedia project *Musica o Muerte* captures the phenomenon of liberation through music in photography as well as in video. *Cuba Libre* presents conversations with Cuban ex-political prisoners in cooperation with Unión de Expresos Políticos Cubanos.

La Otra Cuba was exhibited at the Florida International University in Miami in 2016 with an opening lecture by Jacques Rupnik, organised by Prof. Martin Palous. The series was also exhibited as part of *Day for Cuba* in Prague, organised by *People in Need Foundation*. Hana co-operated on documentary film *Unfinished Dialogue between Vaclav Havel and Osvaldo Payá* organised by Florida International University and Vaclav Havel Initiative / Knight Foundation, which premiered at the Forum 2000 Conference in Prague in 2016. As part of the Forum 2000 Conference, Hana organised presentation of her Cuba work accompanied by discussion with members of *Cubalex*, Havana-based organisation of human rights lawyers, together with political activists from Miami and members of *Human Rights Foundation* in New York.

Hana's photographs have been published worldwide - Books: *Czech Photography of the 20th Century*, Kant Publishing | *Photobox: The Essential Collection - 250 Images You Need To See*, Thames & Hudson | *New York: A Photographer's City*, Rizzoli / Marla Hamburg Kennedy, Magazines and Media: National Geographic, Newsweek, Conde Nast Traveller, Ego Magazine, Reflex, Echo, Radio 1, Russia TV, CNN, among others).

Mrs. Jakrlova's curatorial endeavours include the *L.A.F.: Laughter and Forgetting International Photography Project*, organised in co-operation with New York University in Prague and FAMU Film School in 2009 to mark the 20th anniversary of the Velvet Revolution and aimed at supporting artists living in post-totalitarian countries. The international photography project was exhibited worldwide and supported photographer in Tbilisi Georgia, and premiered at the Forum 2000 Conference in 2009.

Hana's lectures and workshops include New York University Tisch School, International Centre of Photography in NY,

Museum of Contemporary Arts in Moscow, Museum of Photography in Charleroi Belgium, Anglo-American University in Prague and photography workshop at Zero Art Space in Rangoon in Burma (with FAMU Prague).

Mrs. Jakrlova's photography works have been exhibited and published world-wide (Art Basel Miami, Paris Photo, Photo London, Moscow Month of Photography, The Browse Fotofestival Berlin, Bratislava Month of Photography, Prague Biennial, Brescia Photography Festival, Encontros da Imagem in Braga, Museum of Photography Charleroi, Museum of Contemporary Arts Moscow, International Center of Photography Museum in New York and *Eric Franck Fine Art*, London; *Robert Berman Gallery*, Los Angeles; *PDBN Gallery*, Dallas, among others) and won awards at various photography competitions and festivals. Her photographs are parts of numerous public and private collections.

www.hanajakrlovaphoto.com

www.hanajakrlovastudio.com

Hana Jakrlova - Photography books:

Hana Jakrlova, Josef Chuchma, opening word Vaclav Havel: *In the Meantime: Europe*

Photography book, published by Kant Publishing, Schilt Publishing, Eric Franck Fine Art in English, Dutch, Czech: ISBN 10: 8086970175 ISBN 13: 9788086970172, 2008

Hana Jakrlova, Marvin Heiferman: *Big Sister* Photography book, published by Images en Manoeuvres, Eric Franck Fine Art in French, English: ISBN-10: 2849951846, ISBN-13: 978-2849951842, 2011

Hana Jakrlova - Cuba Publications:

Lyric Levin, Hana Jakrlova: *Cuba's World of Fantasy*, CNN Edition, 2015

Odnřej Formánek, Hana Jakrlova: Cuba - *Pravěcí ještěři a George Bush*, Ego Hospodářské noviny, 2015

Hana Jakrlova: *Kuba před úsvitem*, Echo 24 Magazine , 2015

Jiří Holubec, Hana Jakrlova: *Punk na Kubě*, Cili Chili Magazine, 2016

Ondřej Formánek: *Hana Jarklová - Interview*, Zátiší, Radio 1, 2016

Daniel Anýž, Hana Jakrlova: *Musica o Muerte*, Newsweek Czech Republic, 2016

Oskars Kastens:

Biography

Mr. Oskars Kastens has a journalist's background. He has worked in both print and electronic media. He established the Latvian Public TV (LTV) office in Brussels and ran it from 1998 to 2001. In 2002, he joined Latvia's First Party and contributed to the party's election campaign, which the result being 10% of the seats in Latvian Parliament. From 2002 to 2010 Mr. Kastens served eight years as a Member of the Latvian Parliament, where he chaired the Human Rights and Public Affairs, as well as European Affairs committee. While an MP, Mr. Kastens worked on human rights, international parliamentary cooperation, economic development and Latvia's EU accession process. From 2006 to 2008, he served as Latvia's Minister for Social Integration, responsible for ethnic minorities living in Latvia and for coordinating anti-discrimination policy, as well as participating in election observation missions to Azerbaijan, Ukraine, Montenegro and Belarus. Since 2010 Mr. Kastens has worked as an international expert with EU, UNDP, WB and Council of Europe in assistance projects in Albania,

Kosovo, Moldova, Armenia, Moldova, Georgia and other countries. Since 2014 Mr. Kastens regularly participates in EU Election Observation Missions around the world as a short-term observer. He is a Member of the Advisory Board of the Global Panel Foundation.

Part III: Organisation

Program overview

Sunday, Nov. 22

18:00-21:00 **Reception with leaders of the Cuban democratic opposition**

at the residence of Mrs. Ingrid R., Berlin

Monday, Nov. 23:

10:00-14:00 **"Cubans meet Bundestag"** Informal debate session and Lunch with Cuban opposition members and staffers of the Bundestag

at the Restaurant "Habel am Reichstag", Berlin

19:00-22:00 **Public Policy Dinner with Guest of Honor Mr. Boris Luis Santa Coloma,**

Journalist and Founder of "Radio Cuba Dialoga" and Cuban dissidents

at the Casino of Konzerthaus Berlin

Tuesday, Nov 24:

13:00-15:30 **Public Policy Lunch** with Cuban dissidents at the Berlin-Brandenburg Academy of Science and Humanities

15:30-19:00 **Panels** with Cuban opposition members and dissidents at the Berlin-Brandenburg Academy of Science and Humanities

19:30-21:00 **Reception and cultural event** at the Embassy of the Czech Republic, Berlin

Overview of Agenda Nov 24

Public Policy Lunch 1 pm -3.30 pm

Human rights as barometer of change – Experiences of former German and Cuban dissidents? (before main dish)

Human rights as playing field of the antagonism between Cuba and the West? (after main dish)

Opening statement Reinhard **Weißhuhn**,

Robert-Havemann-Society

Roundtable session I 3.30 pm – 5.15 pm

10 years of "Raulismo": Does Western cooperation with the regime delay Cuban reforms?

Opening statement Hon. Markus **Meckel**,

Foreign Minister (Ret.)

Roundtable session II 5.15 pm – 7 pm

Cuba's way ahead:

Painful evolution or peaceful revolution?

Opening statement Hon. Dr. Martin **Palouš**,

Czech Deputy Foreign Minister (Ret.)

Voices of Today´s Cuba

The Global Panel Foundation, The Prague Society for International Cooperation, the Czech Centre and People in Need

invite you to

a cultural evening & reception

with special guests and musicians from Cuba

24 November 2015, 19.30

Embassy of the Czech Republic

Wilhelmstraße 44, 10117 Berlin

Programme

19:30 **Official opening** (cinema hall)

Prof. Marc S. Ellenbogen

Chairman, Global Panel Foundation,

President, Prague Society for International Cooperation

Dr. Martin Palouš

Czech Deputy Foreign Minister (Ret.)

International Platform for Human Rights in Cuba

Markus Meckel

Former Minister of Foreign Affairs

Michael Žantovský

Director of the Václav Havel Library

20:.15 **Exhibition** (foyer)

Work of the Czech organization People in Need (Člověk v tísni) on Cuba

Reception in the presence of special guests from Cuba (foyer)

21:00 **Contemporary Cuban music** (concert hall)

Global Panel Foundation

The Global Panel Foundation works primarily behind the scenes and off-the-record in support of governments, institutions and the private sector. It was founded in 1989 in the Netherlands by Bas Spuybroek and billionaire Frans Lurvink, with the support of then Dutch Foreign Minister Hans van den Broek. In 1998, Global Panel moved its primary office to Berlin, and has since developed operations in Copenhagen, New York, Prague, Sydney and Toronto. Through its network of former ranking government, academic and private sector personalities, Global Panel is well-equipped to facilitate solutions in conflict areas around the world. Global Panel does not take funding from governments. Global Panel has partnered with the Prague Society to annually present the Hanno. R. Ellenbogen Citizenship Award for High Service to Central and Eastern Europe. Recipients have included Vaclav Havel, Madeleine Albright, the Dali Lama and King Michael of Romania. The financial portion of the Award (nearly $10,000) is passed by the recipient to a young person at the beginning of their career. www.globalpanel.org

1. GLOBAL PANEL

1.1 GLOBAL PANEL WORLDWIDE

Marc S. Ellenbogen (Chair, Worldwide)
President, The Prague Society; Founding Trustee, Democratic Expat Leadership Council, U.S. Member of the National Advisory Board, U.S. Democratic Party (2004 -2010)
Hon. Juergen Chrobog, *(Vice Chair, Worldwide) Vice Chair, Board of Directors, BMW Stiftung Herbert Quandt fmr. Deputy Foreign Minister, Germany (2001-2005) fmr. Ambassador to the United States, Germany (1995-2001)*
Dr. Jochen Wittmann *(Vice Chair)*
frm. Director, Dr.-Ing. h.c. F. Porsche AG, Stuttgart
Dr. Kai Gregor Klinger (Treasurer)
Senior Vice President - Investor Relations, Corporate Finance & M&A, RHOEN-KLINIKUM AG
Jens Geitmann
Vice President, The Prague Society; Co-Founder & Managing Director, TriStone Partners
Hon. Klaus Peter Klaiber, KCMG
fmr. Asst. Secretary General of NATO; Ambassador to Australia, Germany
Dr. Vera Lieberwirth
Attorney-at-Law (Germany)
Hon. Jens Hald-Madsen (Chair, Nordic Countries)
fmr. Commissioner for the Danish National Guard; fmr. Vice-Chair, Defense Committee, Danish Parliament

Katja Tobiasz
Entrepeneur and Businesswoman, Mannheim
Ingrid Rexrodt & **Hon. Dr. Günter Rexrodt**, *MP (In Memoriam) fmr. Minister of Trade and Economics, Germany*
Hon. Markus Meckel
frm. President of the German War Graves Commission; fmr. Foreign Minister of the GDR
Hon. Doris Barnett (until June 2013)
German Bundestag, Berlin, Co-Founder, Global Panel Foundation e.V.

1.2 GLOBAL PANEL AUSTRALASIA

Sir Donald C. McKinnon, ONZ, GCVO (Chair)
Commonwealth Secretary General(2000-2008); Deputy P.M. and fmr. Foreign Minister, New Zealand
Hon. Philip Ruddock, MP (Vice-Chair)
Attorney General (2003-2007); Minister for Immigration (1997-2003), Australia
Stewart Young (Treasurer)
Executive Director, Hill Young & Associates
Daniel Street (Secretary)
Reporter, National Nine News
Amb. Winston Cochrane
fmr. Ambassador of New Zealand to Germany, Switzerland, and Saudi Arabia
Marc S. Ellenbogen (Chair, Worldwide)
President, The Prague Society; Founding Trustee, Democratic Expat Leadership Council, U.S.
Bonnie Faulkner
Assistant to the Board of Directors, Australia

Hon. Sen. John Faulkner (Member Emeritus)
Minister of Defense, Australia; Special Minister of State, Australia; Cabinets Secretary;Vice-President of the Executive Council;
Hon. Bob Carr
fmr. Vice Chair Global Panel Australasia, fmr. Foreign Minister; Premier NSW
Warren Reed
Author and Commentator
Hon. Sen. Arthur Sinodinos
Cabinet Secretary, Australian Federal Government
Ezekiel Solomon
Partner, Allens Arthur Robinson; Vice-Chair, International Antitrust Law Committee
Prof. Peter Walls
Deputy-Chair, Victoria University of Wellington
Baron Peter von Fritz
Chairman, Global Access Partners; Managing Director, TCG Group

1.3 GLOBAL PANEL AMERICA

Hon. Barbara J. McDougall (Chair, America)
fmr. Foreign & Finance Minister, Canada
Sir Malcom Rifkind, MP (Vice Chair)
former Defense and Foreign Secretary, UK
Hon. Dov S. Zakheim (Vice Chair)
fmr. V.P., Booz Allen Hamilton; Under Secretary of Defense (2001-2004), USA

Yossef Bodansky (Director)
Senior Advisor, Congressional Task Force on Terrorism and Unconventional Warfare (Director 1988-2004), USA
Marc S. Ellenbogen (Chair, Worldwide)
President, The Prague Society; Founding Trustee, Democratic Expat Leadership Council, U.S.
Robert G. Seasonwein, Esq.
fmr. Assistant Chief Counsel, TSA, Department of Homeland Security, USA
General Dieter Stöckmann (ret.)
fmr. Deputy Supreme Allied Commander Europe, SHAPE, NATO, Germany
Martin Walker
Editor-in-Chief Emeritus, United Press International (UPI), UK

2. Supervisory Board

Prof. Dr. Wilhelm Haarmann *(Chair) Principal Partner, Haarmann, Frankfurt*
Dr. Lutz Raettig *(Vice Chair) Chairman, Supervisory Board, Morgan Stanley Bank AG, Frankfurt; Member, Frankfurt City Council*
Hon. Kurt Bodewig, *MP fmr. Minister of Infrastructure and Transportation , Germany*
Herbert Mai, *fmr. Member of the Executive Board, Frankfurt Airport Authority (Fraport), Germany*
Hon. Barbara J. McDougall, PC, CFA, LL.D. *(Chair, Global Panel America) fmr. Advisor, Aird & Berlis; fmr. Foreign & Finance Minister, Canada*

Sir Donald C. McKinnon, ONZ, GCVO *(Chair, Global Panel Australasia) fmr. Commonwealth Secretary General; fmr. Deputy Prime Minister and Foreign Minister, New Zealand*
General Dieter Stöckmann (ret.) *fmr. Deputy Supreme Allied Commander Europe, SHAPE, Germany*
Hon. Philip Ruddock, MP (V.C. GP Aus)
Attorney General (2003-2007); Minister for Immigration (1997-2003), Australia
Sir Malcom Rifkind, MP (V.C. GP USA)
frm. Defense and Foreign Secretary, UK
Hon. Dov S. Zakheim (V.C. GP USA)
fmr. *V.P., Booz Allen Hamilton; Under Secretary of Defense (2001-2004), USA*
Hon. Dr. Günter Rexrodt, *MP (In Memoriam) fmr. Minister of Trade and Economics, Germany*
Ambassador Prof. Dr. Vladimir Lomeiko *(In Memoriam) President, Baden-Baden Foundation; fmr. Press Secretary to Mikhail Gorbachev*

3. Board of Advisors

3.1 GLOBAL PANEL WORLDWIDE

Hans van den Broek
fmr. European Commissioner and Foreign Minister, Netherlands
Dr. Hans-Hermann Bowitz
fmr. Deputy Chief of Staff to Federal President Roman Herzog, Germany
General Wesley Clark
Supreme Allied Commander of NATO (1997-2000)
Ambassador Frantisek Cerny (ret.)
fmr. Czech Ambassador to Germany

Hon. Enrique Báron Crespo, MEP
fmr. President of European Parliament, Spain
General Constantin Degeratu
fmr. National Security Advisor to the President; fmr. Chief of Staff of the Romanian Armed Forces, Romania
Stuart E. Eizenstat
fmr. Deputy Treasury Secretary and Ambassador, USA
Hon. Foreign Minister Gareth Evans (ret.)
President, International Crisis Group, Brussels
Hon. Mark Eyskens, Ph.D. MP
fmr. Prime Minister, Belgium
Souad Mehkennet
Journalist, Washington Post, ZDF – German 2nd Program
Alexander P. van Heeren, MBE
Industrialist, Philanthropist, Honorary Consul of New Zealand
Hon. Mustafa Kamal Kazi
fmr. Ambassador of Pakistan to Russia and fmr. Under Secretary of State
Hon. Oskars Kastēns, MP
Minister for Social Integration, Latvia (2006-2009)
F.W. de Klerk
Nobel Laureate & Statesman, South Africa
Hon. Eduard Kukan, MP
fmr. Foreign Minister, Slovak Republic
Ambassador Melvyn Levitsky (ret.)
fmr. US Ambassador to Brazil and Bulgaria and Assistant Secretary of State, USA
Hon. Sabine Leutheusser-Schnarrenberger, MP
frm. Justice Minister, Germany
Hon. Stefan Mappus
fmr. Governor, The State of Baden-Wuerttemberg, Germany

Hon. Dr. Dr. h.c. mult. Alois Mock
fmr. Vice-Chancellor and Foreign Minister, Austria
Prof. John Palmer, Ph.D.
The Maxwell School; fmr. Public Trustee, fmr. Assist. Secretary
Ambassador Boris D. Pankin (ret.)
fmr. Soviet Foreign Minister and Russian Amb to theUK
Hon. Dr. Joachim Pfeiffer, MP
Energy Spokesman, CDU Parliamentary Group, German Bundestag
Ash Rajan
Director and Chief Investment Officer, Merrill Lynch, New York
Hon. Klaus Dieter Reichardt
fmr. MP Baden-Wuerttemberg State Legislature
Dr. Klaus Riehmer
Cleary Gottlieb Steen & Hamilton LLP, Frankfurt
Dr. Immo Stabreit
fmr. German Ambassador to South Africa, USA, France
Hon. Shyam Saran
Special Envoy to the Prime Minister; fmr. Foreign Secretary, India
Rt. Hon. Cyril Svoboda
fmr. Minister for Legislative Affairs; fmr. Foreign Minister, Czech Republic
Hon. Gheorghe Tinca
Defense Minister and Ambassador (ret.), Romania
Martin Walker
Editor-in-Chief Emeritus, United Press International (UPI), UK

3.2 GLOBAL PANEL AUSTRAL-ASIA

Yossef Bodansky
Senior Advisor, Congressional Task Force on Terrorism and Unconventional Warfare (Director 1988-2004), USA
Amb. Sang-Hoon Cho
Former Ambassador of the Republic of Korea to Australia and Turkey
Professor Margaret Clark
Chair, Political Science, Victoria University of Wellington
Hon. Laurie Ferguson
fmr. Parliamentary Secretary for Multicultural Affairs and Settlement Services, Australia
The Hon. Phil Goff, MP
Leader of the Opposition; fmr. Minister of Defense; fmr. Minister of Foreign Affairs & Trade, New Zealand
Hon. Klaus Peter Klaiber, KCMG
Former Asst. Secretary General of NATO; Ambassador to Australia, Germany
Hon. Jens Hald Madsen, MP (Chair, Nordic Countries)
fmr. Commissioner for the Danish National Guard; fmr. Vice-Chair, Defense Committee, Danish Parliament
Hon. Sandra Christine Nori
frm. Minister for Women, Tourism, Smalll Business, New South Wales, Australia
Hon. Sen. Henry Tsang, MLC
fmr. Parliamentary Secretary to the Premier, NSW;
Hon. Malcolm Turnbull, MP
Prime Minister, Australia
Professor Peter Walls
Chief Executive Officer, New Zealand Symphony Orchestra

3.3 GLOBAL PANEL AMERICA

Hon. Hassan Abouyoub
Chief Foreign Policy Advisor to King Mohamed VI of Morocco;
fmr. Minister of Trade
Hon. Charles C. Adams Jr., Esq.
fmr. U.S. Ambassador to Finland
Hon. Shahid Kamal
fmr. Ambassador of Pakistan to the German; fmr. Ambassador to Sweden, Finland, Estonia and Latvia
Hon. Richard L. Brodsky
fmr. Chairman, Committee on Corporations, Authorities and Commissions, New York State Legislature, USA
Jennifer Brunner Hon. Judge
fmr. Secretary of State, The State of Ohio
Baroness Cox of Queensbury
fmr. Deputy Speaker, House of Lords, UK
Hon. Ján Čarnogurský
fmr. Prime Minister and Minister of Justice, Slovakia
Hon. Paula J. Dobriansky
US Under-Secretary of State for Global Affairs (2001-2008)
Stuart E. Eizenstat
former Deputy Treasury Secretary and Ambassador, USA
Hon. Sen. John Faulkner (Member Emeritus)
fmr. Minister of Defense, Australia; Special Minister of State, Australia; Cabinets Secretary;Vice-President of the Executive Council;
Lord Holme of Cheltenham (*In Memoriam*)
Liberal Peer; Chancellor, University of Greenwich; Business Leader, UK

Major General Bruce M. Lawlor (ret.)
Chief of Staff Department of Homeland Security (2003-2006); Member of the Commission on the Black Sea
Hon. Dan Maffei (Member Emeritus)
Commissioner, Federal Maritime Commission.
fmr. United States Congressman, 25th District of the State of New York
John O'Sullivan
former Special Advisor to Prime Minister Margaret Thatcher; Editor at Large, National Review, UK
Peter Palečka
Senior Executive Director and Secretary of the Board of Directors, Komerční Banka,Czech Republic
Andrés Pastrana Arango
President of Colombia (1998-2002)
Hon. Pavol Paska, MP
President of the Slovak National Assembly (2006 -2010)
Vice Chairman, Smer - Social Democracy Party, and Minority Leader of the National Assembly
Lord Pearson of Rannoch
Independent conservative Peer, Business Leader, UK
Thomas R. Pickering
Vice Chairman, Hills & Company; former Under Secretary of State and Ambassador; former Senior Vice President, Boeing, USA
HRH Prince Radu of Romania
Hon. Philip Ruddock, MP (Vice Chair, Global Panel Australasia)
Attorney General (2003-2007); Minister for Immigration (1997-2003), Australia
Lord Robertson of Port Ellen
Deputy Chairman, TNK-BP plc ; Labour Peer; Former Secretary General, NATO; former Minister of Defense, UK

Hon. Richard Schnepf
fmr. Amb. of Poland to USA; former Deputy Foreign Minister
Hitoshi Tanaka
Senior Fellow, Japan Center for International Exchange (JCIE); former Deputy Foreign Minister, Japan
Zdeněk Tůma
Governor of the Central Bank, Czech Repubic (2000 - 2010)
Hon. Roger Wicker
United States Senator, Mississippi
James Woolsey
fmr. Vice President, Booz Allen Hamilton; Director, CIA (1993-1995)
Henrikas Yushkiavitshus
Assistant Director-General, UNESCO (1990-2001) Lithuania

The Prague Society for International Cooperation

The Prague Society for International Cooperation grew from the underground movement which helped to fight Communism during the Cold War. The Society believes the perspectives of others are of particular importance to Central and Eastern Europe, whose talents, skills and energy have yet to be fully realized. The ambitions of the days following the collapse of Communism have faded. There is a reluctance to share information and work towards a common goal. Private gain dominates public interest. Corruption is rampant. Suspicion of innovation and foreign influence is endemic. Since her founding by a diverse group from the Czech Republic, Slovakia, Canada, the United Kingdom, the United States, New Zealand and Germany, the Society has focused attention on elements in society who would block fair playing fields and open development. The Prague Society has a reputation for being straight-forward, honest and nonpartisan and respected by opinion leaders.

www.praguesociety.org

THE HONORARY PRESIDENT

Frederik Willem de Klerk - Nobel Laureate & Statesman

THE PRESIDENT

Marc S. Ellenbogen President, Prague Society; Chair, Global Panel Foundation

VICE-PRESIDENTS

Arthur Braun - BPV Braun Partners, Managing Partner

Jens Geitmann Co-Founder & Managing Director, TriStone Partners

Bert Stiers Managing Director, Stiers & Co

Jonathan Wilkinson Founder; Discovery Group;

MEMBERS

Ensour Abdullah - Prime Minister of Jordan (2012-2016)

Norbert Auerbach - Former president and C.E.O of United Artists, a major motion-company (In Memoriam)

Daniel Biguine Corporate Chairman & Art Collector

Cornel Boda – Chairman and CEO, Cobra

Yossef Bodansky - Senior Advisor, Congressional Task Force on Terrorism and Unconventional Warfare, Director (1988-2004)

Ivan Boháček - Publisher & Editor of Vesmír, Natural Sciences Journal of the Academy of Sciences

Sean Bradley – fmr. Director of International Business Development, GeoPost; fmr. CEO, DHL, CZ

Dallosch Burkhard - COO, Asset Management, Deka Immobilien GmbH

Vojtich Cepl - Justice of the Constitutional Court, (In Memoriam)

Tomáš Chrenek - Chairman, Moravia Steel Group.

Caroline Cox; Baroness of Queensbury - Member and Former Deputy Speaker of the British House of Lords. Founder, The Humanitarian Aid Relief Trust (HART).

Barbara Day - Former Executive Director of the Jan Hus Educational Foundation

Marietta Delgado - Former Executive Director, Volvo Cars Czech Republic

Jiřina Dienstbierová - Director, Czech Council on Foreign Relations

Thomas Dine – fmr. President, Radio Free Europe/ Radio Liberty (ret.) Israel Policy Forum (IPF), Former Senior Policy Advisor. President AFoCR

Jessica Douglas-Home - Chairman, Mihai Eminescu Trust, London/Bucharest

Vera Egermayer – fmr. Honorary Consul of New Zeland; Co-founder, European Association of Jewish Child Survivors of the Holocaust

Roger Errera (Member Emeritus) - Honorable member of the French Conseil

Randall Filer - Chairman of the Board/President - CERGE-EI Foundation

José Eduardo Fleming - Former Ambassador of Argentina to Czech Republic

Štefan Füle - Former European Commissioner, fmr. Ambassador and Dep. Def. Min.

Peter Gottwald – Former Ambassador of Germany to Switzerland - Former Commissioner for Disarmament and Nuclear Issues

Michele Green - Owner, New Europe Media, Bucharest, Prague and Istanbul

William Harter - Managing Partner, Wagenhofer spol sro. Frm. Vice-President, Proctor & Gamble, Europe.

Eliska Hasek Coolidge - Former special assistant to five US Presidents, Alumna, Georgetown School of Foreign Service

Markus H. Hermann - Managing Director, MAROM, s.r.o., CR

Jakub Hladík - Former Head of Office for Czech President Václav Havel; Executive Secretary to the PPF Board

Thilo Hoffmann - Weinhold Legal, Partner

Aardse Jaap - Phillips, Head; Managing Director, Ardsco, sro (ret.)

Jan Jůn - Radio Free Europe/Radio Liberty, London

Hon. Peake Karolina - Former Deputy Prime Minister and Defense Minister

Hon. Jan Kasl - Architect; Mayor of Prague (1998-2002)

Hon. Jeremy Kinsman - Former Canadian Diplomat and Ambassador. Lead author of the Diplomat's Handbook for Democracy Development Support

MGen Rostislav Kotil – fmr. Advisor on Defence Policy and Strategy, Czech Ministry of Defense

Elisabeth Princess Lobkowicz - Business Consultant

John Marks, OBE - Co-Director, Educational Research Trust, UK (In Memoriam)

Mark Martin - Manager and Director, Amnesty International Czech Republic

Roman Mentlik - Manager, S&D Financial Services Leader, IBM

Bear Midkiff - Midkiff Consultancy Services, Director

Martin Moulis - Former Deputy Minister of Justice

Hon. Petr Nečas - Former Czech Prime Minister

Hon. Edvard Outrata - Former Vice-President of Senate, Former President of the Czech Statistical Office

Hon. Peter Palečka - Senior Executive Director, Komerční banka, a.s., fmr. Ambassador

Hon. Dr. Martin Palouš - Former Permanent Representative of the Czech Republic to the United Nations in New York

Hon. Pavol Paška - Former Speaker of the Parliament of Slovakia; President of the Slovak National Assembly (2006 - 2010; since 2012), fmr. Vice Chairman, Smer - Social Democracy Party, Minority Leader of the National Assembly

Hon. José Júlio Pereira Gomes – Former Ambassador of the Portuguese Republic

Brod Peter – Honorary member, Writer; Former Editor, BBC Czech Service

Petr Polievka - Director, Deonamedi

George P. Schmolz – fmr. Head of the ARD Prague studios

Hon. Theodor Sedgwick - former US Ambassador to Slovakia

Hon. Pavel Seifter - Former Ambassador to the United Kingdom; Former Foreign Policy Advisor to President Havel

Dr. Martin Jan Stransky - Physician, Poliklinika Narodni

Marian Švejda – fmr. Representative of News Corporation, Czech and Slovak Republics

Hon. Cyril Svoboda - Former Foreign Minister; Diplomatic Academy, Director

Hon. Koichi Takahashi - Former Ambassador of Japan to the Czech Republic; Advisor, MSIG Mitsui Sumitomo Insurance Co. Chair, Czech-Jap Business Asn.

Hon. Jindřich Tomáš - Former Deputy Defense Minister, Czech Republic

Jana Baroness von Hildprandt Germenis - President; Association of Castle Owners, (AMHZ)

Chatelaine of Castle Blatná, Czech Republic

Supporting Institutions

International Platform for Human Rights in Cuba (IPHRC)
IPHRC is a US non-for profit organization based in Miami closely cooperating with Vaclav Havel Center at Stephen Green School of International and Public Affairs at Florida International University, active in the field of advocacy for human rights, serving as principal liaison with the activists of Cuban civil society organizations both in exile and on the island.[17]

People in Need (PIN) (Czech: *Člověk v tísni*)
PIN is a Czech nonprofit, non-governmental organization that implements humanitarian relief and long term development projects, educational programs, and human rights programs in crisis regions all over the world. ...The organization aims to promote democratic freedom and principles of human solidarity. Since its foundation in 1992, PIN has had a presence in almost 50 countries.[18]

---

[17] Martin Palouš, The Role of Vaclav Havel Legacy Institutions in the Current Cuban Debate and the proposed Cuba-Related Activities in 2016, in this volume.

[18] Retrieved on June 16, 2016 from https:// en. Wikipedia.org /wiki/ People_in_Need_(Czech_Republic).

Vaclav Havel Library (VHL)

VHL is a principal co-ordination center of all Havel-related activities not only in the Czech Republic but around the world (a primary database for research projects, a central hub of all activities in the field of public advocacy, human rights diplomacy).[19]

Czech Centres

Czech Centres (Czech: *Česká centra*) is an organization of the Ministry of Foreign Affairs of the Czech Republic consisting of offices in 22 countries throughout three continents. It was established for the promotion of the Czech Republic's history, culture, language, tourism and trade abroad. It is considered an active instrument of foreign policy of the Czech Republic through public diplomacy.[20]

---

[19] Martin Palouš, The Role of Vaclav Havel Legacy Institutions in the Current Cuban Debate and the proposed Cuba-Related Activities in 2016, in this volume. See also VHL, http://www.vaclavhavel-knihovna.org/en.

[20] Retrieved on October 21, 2016 from https:// en. wikipedia.org/ wiki /Czech_Centres

Further reading

Bramnick, Kayla M. Germany's yesterday is Cuba's tomorrow: Comparing the German democratization to the Cuban transformation, Liberty University Law Review, Vol. 10:1, 2015, pp. 1-44.

Bye, Vegard. The Politics of Cuban Transformation – what Space for Authoritarian Withdrawal? (NUPI Working Paper 818), Oslo: Norwegian Institute of International Affairs, 2013, pp. 1-41.

Cave, Damien. The Cuban Evolution, The New York Times, March 2, 2014, p. SR1. Retrieved on November 21, 2015. From: http://www.nytimes.com/2014/03/02/sunday-review /the-cuban-evolution.html.

Gershman, Carl. Castro: Revolutionary or Tyrannical Demagogue? World Affairs Journal, 2016. Retrieved on January 4, 2017. From: http://www.worldaffairsjournal. org/ article/castro-revolutionary-or-tyrannical-demagogue.

Gonzalez, Mike. The Worst of All Possible Cubas, The American Interest, Summer (May/June), 2015, pp. 33-39.

Gratius, Susanne. Zehn Jahre »Raulismo« in Kuba - Verzögert die internationale Anerkennung den Reformprozess?, SWP-Aktuell 91, November 2015, pp.1-7. Retrieved on November 21, 2015. From: http://www.swp-berlin.org/de/publikationen/swp-aktuell-de/swp-aktuell-detail/article/zehn_jahre_raulismo_in_kuba.html.

Grenier, Yvon. Not Free But Comfy: Cuban Art Between State and Market, Literal 35, posted on March 9, 2014 at 1:03 am, n.p. Retrieved on January 16, 2017. From: http://literalmagazine.com/not-free-but-comfy-cuban-art-between-state-and-market/.

Human Rights Watch. Cuba – Country Summary, January 2015, pp.1-6. Retrieved on November 21, 2015. From: https://www.hrw.org/world-report/2015/country-chapters/cuba.

Österreichischer Rundfunk ORF. Dutzende Festnahmen in Kuba am Tag der Menschenrechte, published on December 11, 2015. Retrieved on December 11, 2015. From: http://orf.at/stories/2313928/.

Poushter, Jacob. Latin Americans Approve of U.S. Re-establishing Diplomatic Ties with Cuba, Pew Research Center, July 21, 2015.

Rytz, Henriette M. Ethnic Interest Groups in US Foreign Policy-Making: A Cuban-American Story of Success and Failure, New York City: Palgrave Macmillan 2013.

Vivanco, José Miguel. Lifting the Embargo Means Cuba Can No Longer Play Victim, Time, December 19, 2014. Retrieved on November 21, 2015. From: http://time.com/3642109/us-cuba-embargo/.

Part IV:

Remarks for the Cuban National Reunion

Martin Palouš: The Speech at the Final Dinner of Cuban National Reunion

San Juan, Puerto Rico

Saturday, August 15, 2015 (The Feast of the Assumption of the Blessed Virgin Mary)

Dear Cuban Friends,

I

It is a really honor for me to be with you here tonight – Catholics celebrating the Feast of the Assumption of the Blessed Virgin Mary - and be invited to address you at the final dinner of your national meeting. Let me first thank the organizers for their excellent work and applaud all of you for your contributions to this extremely interesting debate I have had an opportunity to observe and reflect on during the past three days.

The Declaration of San Juan, you have just adopted and which will be read here tonight, is undoubtedly an important step forward, in your very long journey to get over the totalitarian regime – in power over 56 years now – and finally restore democracy in Cuba and bring freedom and prosperity to the Cuban people. The fact that you speak in it in one voice, both Cubans from the island and exile - regardless the differences of points of view you may have, based on your life experience, religious creed or political orientation - means a lot, indeed, and is sending out a powerful message not only to the Cuban nation, but to the whole world.

I am perfectly aware that the debate on the future of Cuba is primarily your Cuban internal affair; that no one else but you Cubans are in charge here to formulate strategies; to make plans; to implement decisions and bear responsibility for their outcomes. But allow me to step into your conversation for a moment and share with you a couple of thoughts from my outside perspective.

II

I have been already introduced here tonight – actually I forgot to thank you……for your kind words – but let me add a couple of further comments departing from my personal encounters with the Cuban problem in the past.

I remember well my first visit to South Florida to meet with the representatives of Cuban American community in 1990, when out of sudden, after the decades spent in the cage of totalitarian system, the world widely opened for us and we were given an opportunity to travel abroad.
Everybody I talked to in these “fair, well-spoken days”, seemed to be expecting then that the fall of communism in East Central Europe would cause the same opening in Cuba (the Soviet Union was withdrawing from the island, and the United States just ninety miles away); that it was just a matter of time before another, in this case imaginary Berlin Wall built by Fidel Castro, would collapse, but simply it didn’t happen. Instead, the “special period” brought aggravated hardships on ordinary Cubans and just some adjustments of the existing system reacting to the worsened economic situation. The power structure of the regime, however, remained intact and the “Cuban Revolution” survived. Why?

I am sure that you know the reasons much better than I do. Let me just add a few comments based on our Central

European experience of transition. There were “things”, for sure, we had to do at home and no one could do them for us, when we started as dissidents assembled in the Charter 77 our journey to freedom, calling for the dialogue with the government about human rights. As members of nations living in the territory traditionally exposed to the geopolitical influences of bigger powers, we could hardly succeed in our liberation without an enabling international environment. In order to be able to re-open our societies and get rid of our own Czechoslovak totalitarian government we had to be released from the Babylonian captivity in the Soviet Empire where we got into after the Second World War.

Were we here entirely dependent on the evolution of relationships between the superpowers? Could we pursue some sort of foreign policies of our own as an independent human rights initiative, to influence our situation and achieve our goals?

My answer is: yes we could, but it required not only persistence, but also realistic assessment of the existing international situation, knowledge of mechanisms and procedures of inter-state relations, especially in the area of human rights, the art of negotiation and coalition building...., in short the overall effectivity of our actions. What offered us an opportunity to make our case in the international realm in the 1970s and

1980 were the policies of "détente" in Europe; all major powers had interest to participate at, so called Helsinki Process which was to transform the Cold War confrontation into cooperation, the "peaceful relationships between states with different social and political systems."

There was a key condition if we wanted not to fail with our cause: the recognition of all the parties, including the countries of the Soviet bloc, that fundamental human rights and freedoms had to be respected and that the independent voices of civil society had to be recognized as legitimate partners in this process. It was a tough struggle, but with the help of our international friends and allies - the United States decided to lead here by example - we got this recognition in the end of the day and became the players on the international scene in the process which succeeded to decrease the tension in the relationships between the East and the West and culminated in our 1989 Velvet Revolution.

III

What I would like to stress in my second hindsight is the importance of international solidarity the most important lesson we learned in the years of struggle. After we ourselves were liberated from the communist yoke we tried to pay back our debt as much as we could when formulating the new foreign policies of our now democratic state. It is actually this sentiment and this conviction what has created the firm bond existing till today between the Czech and the Cuban people, in spite of the geographic distance and many differences between our histories, cultures, mentalities, habits and forms of expression. Iit is why we are on your side in your struggle for democracy in Cuba, and we will remain to be with you in the future.

To illustrate my point I will read you from a historical document: from a statement I delivered as the head of the Czech delegation in Geneva in April 1999 under the occasion of the 55th session of Commission for Human Rights as one of the two coauthors of the draft resolution on the human rights situation in Cuba.

I believe, the arguments formulated in this statement introducing our draft resolution - criticizing the Cuban government for the non-compliance with its international obligations and defending Cuban dissidents and their cause of human rights - remain valid till today.

And just to argue that good things can occasionally happen within the international community of states: we didn't only make our case in front of the international audience worked hard by the experienced and savvy team of Cuban diplomats. We won it, after the United States had lost in the same struggle in the previous year! It was a small, but still a sweet victory in a very difficult international environment over the arrogant and overly too self-confident totalitarian regime.

Madam Chairperson,

".....Our action is based on the recognition of and the respect for the elementary standards of the International Bill of Rights, valid for all members of the international community....If we believe that human rights are indivisible and of a universal nature, we must be ready to defend them not only when our own fate and well-being are at stake, but

also when others are being deprived of them, - in whichever part of the world.

The co-authors, the Czech Republic and Poland, have strong reasons to take this step. These reasons largely stem from their own historical experience with the same totalitarian system as the one now practiced in Cuba. Former dissidents learned to appreciate the value of support from the democratic world.... when they were themselves persecuted not so long ago. Our commitment to help other people persecuted for human rights originates from there. ......

The resolution, while being critical, is definitely not confrontational. Its underlying philosophy is the promotion of international dialogue and cooperation. Its aim is not only to condemn what we consider as evident and blatant violations of human rights, but also to signal the readiness to extend a helping hand to Cuba. The international community declares here unequivocally its sincere will to assist Cuba in developing a more pluralistic society and a more efficient economy.

Let me now make a few additional points on behalf of the Czech Delegation. After all, it was in Prague, and not anywhere else, that the idea to initiate this resolution came from. For us, Czechs, Cuba is not an abstract or an exotic term, but a country known to many people from intensive contacts before the fall of the Berlin Wall in 1989. There is a long tradition of good relations between Czechs and Cubans and our motion is definitely not meant to throw it away.

Nevertheless, we made our own bitter experience with a political regime which paid no respect to human rights and kept our whole society closed for decades. We learned that there can be no real development, no economic prosperity, and no well-being of the people, no constructive dialogue, and no active involvement, without democracy, without the rule of law, without the honest and principled policy in the field of human rights.

Our experience makes us to believe that it is the internationalization of human rights that creates a favorable environment for peaceful international politics. And not only that: it is again the internationalization of human rights, that represents a "sine qua non" condition for efficient, rational and at the same time just forms of international economic cooperation. Our position has a clear implication: Isolation, any form of political or economic "containment", the absence of communication, the language of confrontation cannot bring us closer to our goal which is universal respect for human rights, but also economic and social development. Isolation and the feeling of hostile encirclement provide a fertile ground for the justification of repression. We have to commit ourselves and must be able to find other, more creative and more helpful approaches.

The main reasons for its submission, at least on the Czech side can be characterized with (the French philosopher) Pascal as the "reasons of the heart" (les raisons du coeur): Ten years ago, the Czech dissidents (and one can easily add the Slovak, Polish, Hungarian and many other dissidents from East-Central Europe) were in a similar situation as many individuals in Cuba today and they highly appreciated any expression of international solidarity. It is not only difficult to forget that, but what else but a true spirit of solidarity and cooperation can be recommended as the basic principle of action for the international community?

Let me conclude with President Havel's words: "Only the voting result will show to what extent we will have succeeded in our intentions. Whatever the outcome, our conviction that his step is the right thing will remain unchanged. We can imagine ourselves in the position of those whose cause we are advocating. Our own past history supplies ample evidence that far too often the roles of the defenders and the defended can be reversed."

I believe I can conclude with these words, from 16 years, as well. As you well know, I am not diplomat any more but I can assure you: I am still trying in my current capacities - as Director of Vaclav Havel Program for Human Rights and Diplomacy at Florida International University in Miami, President of Vaclav Havel Library Foundation in New York, and last, but not least President of International Platform for Human Right in Cuba – to pay back our lasting debt in the field of international solidarity: to help your dignified cause to the best capabilities of all these institutions I am associated with – to share with you our experience, to be your honest and reliable partner in an on-going dialogue, to make your efforts on the international scene more effective, and first of all to assist you to win.

Thank you for your attention.

Martin Palouš:

El discurso en la cena de final del Encuentro Nacional de Cuba

San Juan, Puerto Rico

Sábado, 15 de agosto 2015

(La fiesta de la Asunción de la Bienaventurada Virgen María)

Queridos amigos Cubanos,

I

Es realmente un honor para mí estar con ustedes aquí esta noche – de la fiesta de la Asunción de la Bienaventudura Virgen María - y ser invitado de dirigirme a ustedes en la cena final de su encuentro nacional. Quiero dar las gracias en primer lugar a los organizadores por su excelente trabajo y aplaudo a todos ustedes por sus contribuciones a este debate muy interesante que he tenido la oportunidad de observar y reflexionar durante los últimos tres días.

La Declaración de San Juan, que han recien adoptado y que se va a leer aquí esta noche, es sin duda un paso importante hacia adelante, en su viaje muy largo para supercar el régimen totalitario - en el poder más de 56 años - y, finalmente, restaurar la democracia en Cuba y llevar la libertad y la prosperidad para el pueblo cubano. El hecho de que hablan en el documento de una sola voz, ambos cubanos de la isla y el exilio - sin tener en cuenta las diferencias de puntos de vista que pueda tener, en base a su experiencia de vida, religión u orientación política - significa mucho, por cierto, y es el envío de un mensaje de gran alcance no sólo para la nación cubana, sino a todo el mundo.

Estoy perfectamente consciente de que el debate sobre el futuro de Cuba es principalmente un asunto interno de Cuba; que nadie más que ustedes, los cubanos están a cargo aquí para formular estrategias; hacer planes; para poner en práctica las decisions y asumir la responsabilidad por sus resultados. Pero permítame que pase en su conversación por un momento y compartir con ustedes un par de pensamientos desde mi punto de vista externo.

II

He estado ya introducido aquí esta noche - en realidad se me olvidó darle las gracias ...... por sus amables palabras -

pero permítanme añadir un par de comentarios adicionales saliendo de mis encuentros personales con el problema cubano en el pasado.

Recuerdo bien mis primeros encuentros con la comunidad cubano-americana en 1990, cuando de repente, después de las décadas pasados en la jaula del Sistema totalitario, el mundo se abrio ampliamente para nosotros y nos dieron la oportunidad de viajar al extranjero.

Todo el mundo con que yo hablaba en esos días parecía estar esperando entonces que la caída del comunismo en Europa Central Oriental causaría la misma apertura en Cuba (la Unión Soviética se retiraba de la isla y los Estados Unidos sólo 90 a millas); que era sólo una cuestión de tiempo, pero no fue así. En cambio, el "período especial" trajo dificultades agravadas a los cubanos de a pie y tal vez algunos ajustes del Sistema existente al empeoramiento de la situación económica. La estructura de poder, sinembargo, del régimen se mantuvo intacta y la "Revolución Cubana" sobrevivió. Por qué?

Estoy seguro de que ustedes saben las razones mucho mejor que yo. Permitanme añadir mis propios comentarios en base a nuestra propia experiencia de transición Centro Europea. Había "cosas", a ciencia cierta, que teníamos que hacer en casa y nadie podia hacer por nosotros, cuando empezamos como disidentes agrupados en la Carta 77, nuestra marcha hacia la libertad. Como miembros de un grupo de naciones que viven en el territorio tradicionalmente expuesto a las influencias geopolíticas de las potencias más grandes, que dificilmente podíamos tener éxito sin un entorno internacional favorable. Con el fin de ser capaz de volver a abrir nuestras sociedades y deshacerse de nuestro propio gobierno totalitario checoslovaco teníamos que ser liberados de la cautividad Babiloniana en el Imperio Soviético, donde nos metimos como consecuencia de la Segunda Guerra Mundial.

Estábamos aquí sólo dependiendo de la evolución de las relaciones entre las superpotencias? O podríamos seguir algún tipo de política exterior propia, para influir en nuestra situación y lograr nuestros objetivos? Mi repuesta es: Sí podiamos, pero no se requeria solamente la persistencia, sino también la evaluación realista de la situación internacional actual, el conocimiento de los mecanismos y procedimientos de las relaciones interestatales, especialmente en el area de los derechos humanos, el arte de la negociacion y creación de coaliciones... brevemente la efectividad global de nuestras acciones. Lo que nos ofrecio una oportunidad hacer nuestro caso en el ambiente internacional de los años 1970 y 1980 en Europa fueron las políticas de "distensión" en Europa. Todas las grandes potencias tenían interés en participar en el así llamado Proceso de Helsinki, que era transformar la confrontación de la Guerra Fría en cooperacion – las "relaciones pacíficas entre Estados con diferentes sistemas sociales y políticos."

Habia una condición clave si queriamos no fracasar con nuestra causa: el reconocimiento de todas las partes, incluido los países del bloque soviético, que los derechos humanos y las libertades fundamentales tenían que ser respetados y que las voces independientes de la sociedad civil tuvieron que ser reconocidas como socios legítimos en este proceso. Fue una lucha dura, pero con la ayuda de nuestros amigos y aliados internacionales - Estados Unidos decidió liderar con el ejemplo aquí - conseguimos este reconocimiento en el final del día y nos convertimos en los actores en la escena internacional en el proceso que logro disminuir la tencion en las relaciones entre el Este y Oeste y culminó con nuestra Revolución de Terciopelo de 1989.

III

Lo que me gustaría hacer hincapié en mi segunda retrospectiva es la importancia de la solidaridad internacional, la leccion mas importante que hemos aprendido en anos de lucha. Después de que nosotros mismos nos liberamos del yugo comunista tratamos de pagar nuestra deuda tanto como pudimos creando nuevas politicas exteriores de nuestro estado democratico contemporaneo. Es en realidad este sentimiento y esta conviccion que ha creado un lazo firme entre los pueblos Checo y Cubano a pesar de la distancia geográfica y muchas diferencias entre nuestras historias, culturas, mentalidades, costumbres y formas de expresión. Es por que estamos a su lado en su lucha por democracia en Cuba y seguiremos estando con ustedes en el futuro.

Para ilustrar mi punto déjame que les lea de un tipo de documento histórico: desde mi declaración que entregué como jefe de la delegación checa en Ginebra en abril de 1999 con motivo de la 55ª sesión de la Comisión de

Derechos Humanos como uno de los dos coautores del proyecto de resolución sobre la situación de los derechos humanos en Cuba.

Creo que los argumentos formulados en esta declaracion introduciendo nuestro proyecto de la resolucion - criticando al gobierno cubano por el incumplimiento de sus obligaciones internacionales y la defensa de los disidentes cubanos y su causa de los derechos humanos – siguen siendo válidos hasta hoy.

Y sólo para argumentar que las cosas buenas de vez en cuando pueden suceder dentro de la comunidad internacional de Estados: no sólo hicimos nuestro caso frente de la audiencia internacional duramente influenciada por el experimentado y ilustre equipo de los diplomaticos Cubanos. Lo ganamos, después de que Estados Unidos ha perdido en la misma lucha en el año anterior. Una pequeña, pero sigue siendo una dulce victoria en un entorno internacional muy difícil contra el régimen totalitario arrogante y demasiado seguro de sí mismo.

"Señora Presidenta:

. .. Nuestra acción se basa en el reconocimiento y el respeto de las normas elementales de la Carta Internacional de Derechos, válido para todos los miembros de la comunidad internacional ... Si creemos que los derechos humanos son indivisibles y de carácter universal, debemos estar preparados para defenderlos no sólo cuando nuestro propio destino y el bienestar están en juego, sino también cuando los demás se ven privados de ellos, - en cualquier parte del mundo.

Los co-autores, la República Checa y Polonia, tienen fuertes razones para tomar este paso. Estas razones se derivan en gran parte de su propia experiencia histórica con el mismo sistema totalitario como el que ahora se practica en Cuba. Los ex disidentes aprendieron a apreciar el valor del apoyo del mundo democrático .... cuando se vieron perseguidos no hace mucho tiempo. Nuestro compromiso para ayudar a otras personas perseguidas por los derechos humanos se origina a partir de ahí. ......

La resolución, sin dejar de ser crítica, definitivamente no es de confrontación. Su filosofía subyacente es el fomento del diálogo y la cooperación internacional. Su objetivo es no sólo para condenar lo que consideramos violaciónes como evidentes y flagrantes de los derechos humanos, sino también para señalar la disposición a extender una mano de ayuda a Cuba. La comunidad internacional declara aquí inequívocamente su sincere deseo de ayudar a Cuba en el desarrollo de una sociedad más pluralista y una economía más eficiente.

Permítanme ahora hacer algunas observaciones adicionales en nombre de la Delegación checa. Después de todo, fue en Praga, y no en cualquier otro lugar, que la idea de iniciar esta resolución viene. Para nosotros, los Checos, Cuba no es un término abstracto o exótico, sino un país conocido por muchas personas de intensos contactos antes de la caída del Muro de Berlín en 1989. Hay una larga tradición de buenas relaciones entre los Checos y los Cubanos y nuestra moción definitivamente no tiene la intención de tirarla a la basura.

Sin embargo, hemos hecho nuestra propia experiencia amarga con un regimen político que no prestó el respeto a los derechos humanos y mantenia toda nuestra sociedad cerrada durante décadas. Nos enteramos de que no puede haber un verdadero desarrollo, ni la prosperidad económica, y no el bienestar de la gente, no hay diálogo constructivo y sin participación activa, sin democracia, sin el imperio de la ley, sin la política honesta y de principios en el campo de los derechos humanos.

Nuestra experiencia nos hace creer que es la internacionalización de los derechos humanos que crea un ambiente favorable para la política internacional de paz.
Y no sólo eso: es más la internacionalización de los derechos humanos, que representa una condición "sine qua non" para la eficiente, racional y al mismo tiempo justa, forma de cooperación económica internacional. Nuestra posición tiene una clara implicación:

Aislamiento, cualquier forma de "contención" política o económica, la falta de comunicación, el lenguaje de la confrontación no puede llevarnos más cerca de nuestro objetivo, que es el respeto universal de los derechos humanos, pero tambien el desarrollo económico y social. El aislamiento y la sensación de ambiente hostil proporciona un terreno fértil para la justificación de la represión. Tenemos que comprometernos y debemos ser capaces de encontrar otros, más creativos y más útiles enfoques.

Las principales razones de su presentación, al menos en la parte Checa se pueden caracterizar con (el filósofo francés) Pascal como las "razones del corazón" (les raisons du coeur): Hace diez años, los disidentes Checos (y uno puede fácilmente añadir los Eslovacos, Polacos, Húngaros y muchos otros disidentes de Europa centro-oriental) estaban en una situación similar a muchas personas en Cuba hoy y apreciaban mucho cualquier expresión de la solidaridad internacional. No sólo es difícil de olvidar eso, pero ¿qué otra cosa sino un verdadero espíritu de solidaridad y cooperación puede ser recomendado como el principio básico de la acción de la comunidad internacional?

Permítanme concluir con las palabras del presidente Havel: "Sólo el resultado de la votación mostrará hasta qué punto habremos tenido éxito en nuestras intenciones.

Cualquiera sea el resultado, nuestra convicción de que este paso es lo correcto se mantendrá sin cambios. Podemos imaginarnos a nosotros mismos en la posición de aquellos cuya causa defendemos. Nuestra propia historia pasada suministra amplia evidencia de que con demasiada frecuencia las funciones de los defensores y los defendidos se puede revertir."

Creo que puedo concluir con estas palabras, a partir de 16 años, también. Como ustedes bien saben, no soy mas diplomático pero le puedo asegurar que: Todavía estoy tratando en mis capacidades actuales - como Director del Programa de Vaclav Havel para los Derechos Humanos y Diplomacia en la Universidad Internacional de Florida en Miami, Presidente de la Fundación Biblioteca de Vaclav Havel en Nueva York, y por último, el presidente de la Plataforma Internacional para los Derechos Humanos en Cuba - para pagar nuestra deuda duradera en el campo de la solidaridad internacional: para ayudar a su causa digna de las mejores capacidades de todas estas instituciones, para compartir con ustedes nuestra experiencia, para ser su socio en un diálogo en curso, para que sus esfuerzos en la escena internacional sean más eficaz, y en primer lugar para ayudarles a ganar. Gracias por su atención.

Declaration of San Juan*

The first Cuban National Conference met in San Juan, Puerto Rico from August 13 to 15, 2015. Twenty-three organizations from the Cuban archipelago and 32 from the exile participated, duly represented by more than 100 of their leaders. The event was organized by United Cubans of Puerto Rico.

Animating us was the purpose of seeking ways to reconcile the work of the pro-democratic forces with the commitment to restore sovereignty, and all their basic rights, to the Cuban people. To this end, we affirm that to achieve full freedom for the Cuban people and a genuine Rule of Law, the following principles are not negotiable:

- The unconditional release of all political prisoners and the repeal of all laws that violate fundamental freedoms.
- Freedom of speech, press, association, assembly, peaceful demonstration, profession and religion.

- The participation of the people in every decision of the nation, the legalization of all political parties and free and multiparty elections.

The Cuban National Conference also agreed:

1. To work on a the campaign for a binding plebiscite in favor of free, fair and pluralistic democratic elections under conditions that guarantee the sovereignty of citizens.
2. To support and sign the 1988 "Agreement for Democracy."
3. To promote the strategy of nonviolent struggle, facilitating the training of pro-democracy activists in the methods of civil disobedience.
4. To work to demolish the cyber-wall in Cuba and strive so that the domestic opposition has the technological resources to continue citizen mobilization.

Presentations were made on several efforts focused on the material and spiritual progress of the new Cuba, which will be detailed in the second National Cuban Conference.

A Coordinating Liaison Committee was established for a period of six months whose primary task will be to follow up on the agreed points here and communicate them to all organizations, in the spirit of uniting the internal and external opposition.

Today, for us, José Martí's phrase is more relevant than ever and we plan to fulfill it: "Joining together is the watchword."

San Juan, Puerto Rico, August 15, 2015.

*Retrieved on June 29, 2016 from: http://translatingcuba.com/declaration-of-san-juan-cuban-national-conference/ (Excerpt)

Declaratión de San Juan**

Entre los días 13 y 15 de agosto del 2015, sesionó en San Juan, Puerto Rico, el primer Encuentro Nacional Cubano. Participaron 23 organizaciones del Archipiélago y 32 del exilio, debidamente representadas por más de un centenar de sus dirigentes. El evento fue organizado por Cubanos Unidos de Puerto Rico.

Nos animaba el propósito de buscar vías para conciliar la labor de las fuerzas pro-democráticas con el compromiso de restaurar la soberanía a los ciudadanos cubanos y todos sus derechos fundamentales. A esos efectos, afirmamos que, para lograr la libertad plena del pueblo cubano y un genuino estado de derecho, no son negociables ninguno de los siguientes principios:

- La libertad incondicional de todos los presos políticos y la derogación de todas las leyes que atenten contra las libertades fundamentales;
- La libertad de expresión, de prensa, de asociación, de reunión, de manifestación pacífica, de profesión y religión; y

- La participación del pueblo en toda decisión de la nación, la legalización de todos los partidos políticos y las elecciones libres y pluripartidistas.

El Encuentro Nacional Cubano también acordó:

1. Trabajar en la campaña por un plebiscito vinculante en favor de las elecciones libres, justas y plurales, bajo condiciones democráticas, que garanticen la soberanía de los ciudadanos.
2. Respaldar y suscribir el Acuerdo por la Democracia en Cuba, de 1998.
3. Promover la estrategia de la lucha no-violenta, facilitando la capacitación de los luchadores pro-democráticos en las metodologías de la desobediencia civil.
4. Trabajar para derrumbar el muro cibernético en Cuba y esforzarse para que la oposición interna tenga los recursos tecnológicos con los que continuar la movilización ciudadana.

Se expusieron varios trabajos enfocados hacia el progreso material y espiritual de la Nueva Cuba, los que serán definidos en un segundo Encuentro Nacional Cubano.

Se estableció una Comisión Coordinadora de Enlace, por un término de seis meses, cuya tarea fundamental será dar seguimiento a los puntos aquí acordados y comunicárselos a todas las organizaciones, en el espíritu de unir la oposición interna y externa.

Para nosotros tiene hoy más vigencia que nunca la frase martiana que nos proponemos cumplir: "Juntarnos es la palabra de orden".

San Juan, Puerto Rico, 15 de agosto de 2015

**Retrieved on October 21, 2016 from: https://www.cubanet.org/noticias/primer-encuentro-nacional-cubano-declaracion-de-san-juan (Excerpt)

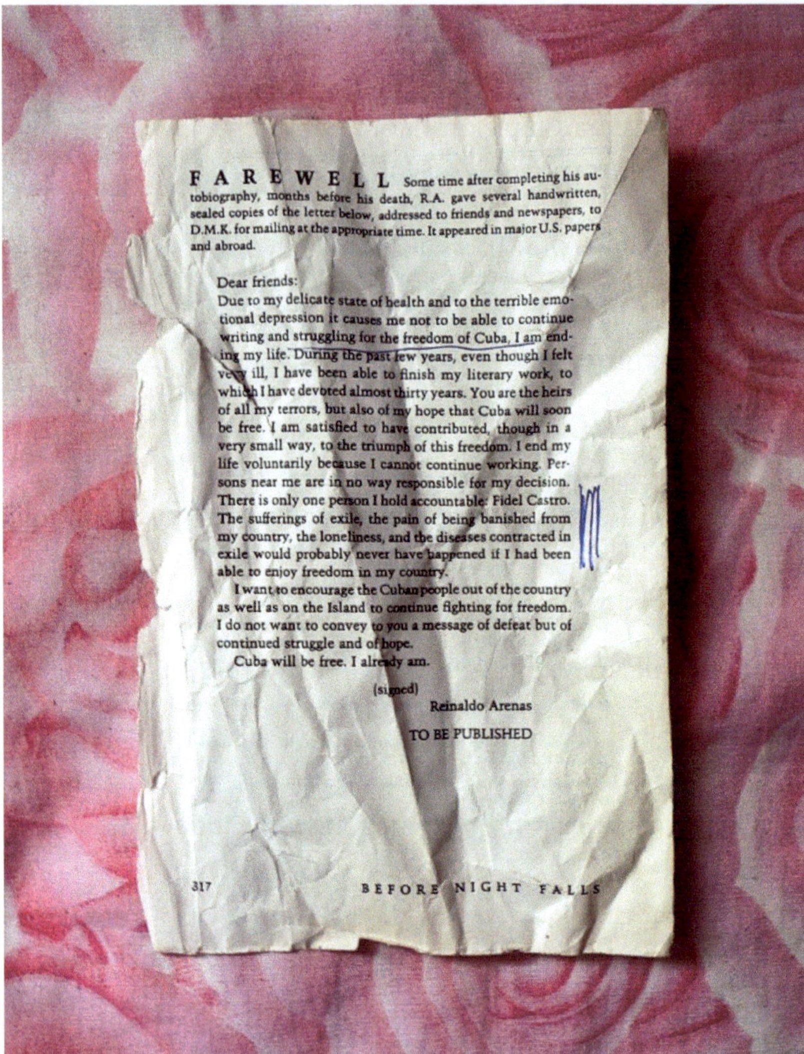

F A R E W E L L Some time after completing his autobiography, months before his death, R.A. gave several handwritten, sealed copies of the letter below, addressed to friends and newspapers, to D.M.K. for mailing at the appropriate time. It appeared in major U.S. papers and abroad.

Dear friends:
Due to my delicate state of health and to the terrible emotional depression it causes me not to be able to continue writing and struggling for the freedom of Cuba, I am ending my life. During the past few years, even though I felt very ill, I have been able to finish my literary work, to which I have devoted almost thirty years. You are the heirs of all my terrors, but also of my hope that Cuba will soon be free. I am satisfied to have contributed, though in a very small way, to the triumph of this freedom. I end my life voluntarily because I cannot continue working. Persons near me are in no way responsible for my decision. There is only one person I hold accountable: Fidel Castro. The sufferings of exile, the pain of being banished from my country, the loneliness, and the diseases contracted in exile would probably never have happened if I had been able to enjoy freedom in my country.

I want to encourage the Cuban people out of the country as well as on the Island to continue fighting for freedom. I do not want to convey to you a message of defeat but of continued struggle and of hope.

Cuba will be free. I already am.

(signed)
Reinaldo Arenas

TO BE PUBLISHED

317 BEFORE NIGHT FALLS

Part V: Impressum

Edited by

Dr. Jochen Wittmann & Prof. Marc S. Ellenbogen

Published by

The Global Panel Foundation

Berlin: Potsdamer Platz | Berlin | Germany

Prague: Vězeňská 5 | 110 00 Prague 1 | Czech Republic

Sydney: Level 39, Australia Square | Sydney | NSW 2000 |

264-278 George Street | Australia

office@globalpanel.org | www.globalpanel.org

The Prague Society for International Cooperation

Prague: Vězeňská 5 | 110 00 Prague 1 | Czech Republic

Phone: +420 722 584 878 | +421 910 901 389

office@praguesociety.org | www.praguesociety.org

Printed and produced by

BoD-Books on Demand, Norderstedt, Germany

ISBN 9783743124523